LIVING IN THE THIRD REICH

In loving memory of

my mother
Josephine Labriola
born 1926 in Lackawanna, New York

and

my mother-in-law
Maria Thomalla
born 1930 in Oberglogau, Silesia

LIVING IN THE THIRD REICH

First-hand Civilian Accounts of Living under the Nazi Regime

Dr Patrick Labriola

Pen & Sword
MILITARY
AN IMPRINT OF PEN & SWORD BOOKS LTD.
YORKSHIRE – PHILADELPHIA

First published in Great Britain in 2025 by
PEN AND SWORD MILITARY
An imprint of
Pen & Sword Books Limited
Yorkshire – Philadelphia

ISBN 978 1 03612 462 5

A CIP catalogue record for this book is available from the British Library.

Typeset in Times New Roman 11.5/14.5 by
SJmagic DESIGN SERVICES, India.
Printed and bound in the UK by CPI Group (UK) Ltd.

The Publisher's authorised representative in the EU for product safety is
Authorised Rep Compliance Ltd., Ground Floor, 71 Lower Baggot Street,
Dublin D02 P593, Ireland.
www.arccompliance.com

For a complete list of Pen & Sword titles please contact
PEN & SWORD BOOKS LIMITED
George House, Units 12 & 13, Beevor Street, Off Pontefract Road,
Barnsley, South Yorkshire, S71 1HN, England
E-mail: enquiries@pen-and-sword.co.uk
Website: www.pen-and-sword.co.uk

or

PEN AND SWORD BOOKS
1950 Lawrence Rd, Havertown, PA 19083, USA
E-mail: uspen-and-sword@casematepublishers.com
Website: www.penandswordbooks.com

Contents

CHAPTER II – ALLIED BOMBINGS

CHAPTER V – THE WESTERN ADVANCE

CHAPTER VI – AFTERMATH OF THE WAR

Preface

I. Idea for the book

My personal introduction to the testimonies of the Third Reich started during family gatherings at the house of my German in-laws. As we sat around the table, conversations often drifted towards recollections of the war years and the hardships endured by those who lived through them. It became increasingly clear to me that these personal narratives were fragile artefacts of history, ones that risked fading into obscurity if not captured and preserved. I began to believe that someone had to take on the responsibility of safeguarding these invaluable historical testimonies, ensuring they would not be lost to the sands of time.

My fascination with the power of oral history deepened in this period while preparing a lecture series at the University of Bonn in Germany. The topic of my course was "America in the 1920s and 30s", and as I delved into my research, I stumbled upon Studs Terkel's groundbreaking work, *Hard Times: An Oral History of the Great Depression*. Terkel's book added an entirely new dimension to my understanding of American history in this period. It showed how the narratives of ordinary people could shed valuable light on the details of historical events in a way that traditional history books often failed to do. I found myself captivated by the rich tapestry of human experiences and emotions that oral history unveiled.

Simultaneously, my curiosity led me to explore the "US Federal Writers' Project", a noble undertaking in the 1930s which included preserving the testimonies of African Americans who had endured slavery, the Civil War, and Reconstruction, as well as testimonies by Native Americans who recalled their way of life before and after the closing of the American West. While the background of these two groups was vastly different from that of Germans who found themselves on the losing side of World War II, the methodology of oral history revealed to me the universal importance of personal testimonies in understanding the intricacies of history. It became evident that, regardless of the circumstances, personal accounts offer a unique and vital perspective on the past. This insight became the driving force behind my mission to document the experiences of those who lived through the era of the Third Reich, and is the foundation upon which this book is built. The personal stories in this oral history fit together like pieces of a mosaic to create a vivid picture of the past, and they come to life through the language of ordinary Germans who experienced the tumultuous era of the Third Reich and the horrors of war.

II. Problems in finding interview partners

The difficulties in finding individuals willing to share their wartime experiences were formidable. The protests by German students in the late 1960s against the war generation had a profound impact on oral history, causing many of those who had lived through the war to close up and refuse to discuss their experiences. The accusations hurled by the youth of that era, coupled with the war generation's inability to provide satisfactory explanations or to defend themselves, further deepened the chasm of silence. In contrast with the "greatest generation" in America, England, France, and Russia, ordinary German soldiers remained a voiceless "silent generation". Consequently, I found myself at an unexpected advantage as a foreigner. As an outsider, I approached these individuals without preconceived judgments or condemnation. I was neither involved in the war nor did I have family members who had died at the hands of the Nazis. In fact, I was willing to listen objectively to their past, and this neutrality seemed to encourage many to open up to me and to share their stories, often for the first time in decades. Personal referrals from my German wife, German friends, and former interview partners also played a crucial role in convincing some individuals to talk to me. Each interview was arduous work which involved sometimes travelling great distances to witnesses' homes, having coffee and cake with them, answering personal questions about my life, and vouching for my honest intentions in conducting the project. Trust is an essential factor when dealing with such sensitive accounts, and personal connections often helped to bridge that trust gap.

The best interviews, I discovered, were those that were not overly rehearsed with a rigid set of questions. Instead, I allowed each witness to speak freely about their experiences, gently guiding the conversation through open-ended questions. This approach allowed the participants to share their memories and emotions more freely. Many of them expressed deep frustration at the disconnection between themselves and their own children. They complained that their offspring had little understanding of where they had been, what they had lived through, or the sacrifices they had made after the war. Another challenge was the fact that it often took many years for some to find the courage to speak about these deeply personal and painful experiences. Some only began to open up in their seventies, eighties, or even nineties, while many others carried their untold stories with them to the grave. The passage of time acted as both a catalyst for sharing and a pressing reminder of the need to record these accounts before they were lost forever due to advancing old age. This book, therefore, stands as a testament to those willing to break their silence, the importance of impartial listening, and the enduring significance of personal testimony in understanding the complex tapestry of history.

III. Methodology

I adopted an unconventional approach in conducting these interviews. Instead of relying on a list of preformulated questions, I engaged in open-ended conversations in German that encouraged the participants to freely recount their memories from childhood to the end of the war. This approach allowed for a more natural and unfiltered narrative, and enabled the witnesses to speak about matters that were important to them. The interviews were conducted in a comprehensive manner, often lasting anywhere from thirty minutes to three hours. The open-ended nature of the discussions permitted them to express themselves at their own pace, ensuring that no crucial details were omitted. Every interview was recorded on tape, later in digital form, and the contents were carefully examined through multiple listening sessions. This process was essential for capturing the full depth of the experiences shared.

Subsequently, I arranged individual passages from the interviews thematically according to the chapters in the book, each covering a specific topic. For example, the first chapter is on the early years of National Socialism, and the second chapter covers the Allied bombings of the civilian population in various German cities. The subsequent chapters include the civilian retreat from the East, the Russian invasion, the Western advance, and the aftermath of the war. Each interview passage is accompanied by a short description of the historical witness, sometimes along with personal documents and photographs. I do not relate my personal feelings in the book, but rather present the information in a mosaic form so that the readers are able to establish their own conclusions. Supplemental or diverging information is provided in footnotes to clarify or elaborate on the testimonies. The book has taken over thirty years to compile, edit, and translate, and comprises over 100 interviews with thousands of hours of recorded documentation.

IV. Interviews, editing, and translation work

In order to create a relaxed atmosphere with each interview partner, I first questioned each person about their name, their place of birth, and their first memories of the Third Reich. From this point onwards, the interviews followed in chronological order, with me asking follow-up questions on important topics. In the initial stages of the oral history project, I sometimes attempted to direct the conversation in a certain direction, or placed emphasis on certain topics such as "the deportation of the Jews", but quickly discovered that each person had their own personal narrative that they wished to follow. This realization caused me to avoid asking too many questions, allowing them to follow their train of thought that they had been holding back for so many years. At times, certain witnesses asked me to turn off the recording device in order to reveal traumatic events that had happened during this period or because they could no longer continue with the interview out of sheer grief. In each interview, however, I tried to capture the quintessential experience that defined their life during this period. Often, it involved one day, one event, or even a single moment.

After having recorded each interview, I was able to listen to it several times, noting down the events discussed and the time of the specific topics in the interview. These unique experiences were then placed in one of several chapters that had emerged in the course of compiling the work. The translation work that followed was the most arduous and time-consuming task. For each testimony, I often had to weigh shades of meaning between certain German terms such as "deportation", "removal", "relocation", and "transport" and also provide unified terminology for historical terms from the Third Reich such as "Reichsarbeitsdienst" or "Waffen-SS". By far the greatest challenge was the identification and transcription of geographic locations and the confirmation of their validity during specific years of the war through the Internet and secondary sources. In the event of diverging or supplemental information, I offer footnotes to the reader for further explanation.

The personal photographs and documents in this work are meant to provide a face to respective interview partners. Many Germans were bombed out and lost all possessions, or their homes fell to occupied territories in the East so that they could not provide me with any personal documents. Some interview partners wished to remain anonymous and even refused the use of their names or in this publication.

The question of subjectivity in compiling, editing, and translating this work also needs to be addressed. One can argue that the questions asked by me in these interviews as well as the subsequent passages chosen for the book constitute my personal narrative which steered the work in a certain direction. This is certainly valid because no book exists without any personal perspective at all. The same holds true for the translation work which compelled me to choose one word over another in describing historical accounts. I was also limited to individuals who were willing to conduct an interview with me. Although I travelled widely and interviewed a vast number of witnesses, I received only a cross-section of average Germans who had experienced the war as children, housewives, soldiers, or uninvolved parties. Although I often tried to interview a representative group from the remaining Jewish community in Germany through friends, associations, and religious groups, there was never any real willingness on their part to speak to me. The same holds true for Germans who held positions of authority in the

Third Reich or were responsible for military command, the deportation of the Jews, or atrocities committed. Therefore, this work comprises interviews with average Germans who had experienced some form of the war. It is therefore not a book about the deportation of the Jews or the well-documented atrocities committed against the Jews. This important research has already been conducted by the Simon Wiesenthal Centre in Vienna, among many others, who are more qualified and competent in this important field.

V. Findings and conclusion

Every German experienced the reality of Nazi Germany in a different manner, depending on the respective year, geographic location, and their gender. The war initiated by the Third Reich ultimately resulted in devastating and lasting repercussions for the German civil population. Not only were millions of civilians killed in the bombings of German cities, but women in particular were often the victims of heinous war crimes involving rape and murder. For example, women in the eastern German territories of Brandenburg, Pomerania, and Silesia were systematically raped by Russian advancing and occupying troops as a means of revenge. Some of these horrendous stories are included in this oral history in Chapter IV ("The Russian Invasion"); however, many women asked that their stories not be published in this book. Moreover, countless German families were driven from their homes in Silesia, the Sudetenland, and the German territories in the East at the end of the war, forced to find a new life in the West. Finally, some civilians shared their experiences at the end of the war at the hands of Allied forces, offering a valuable perspective on what they considered fair treatment during their surrender. Generally, the most favourable assessments were given to the British and Americans. The harshest treatment is often associated with Russian forces.

Many historical witnesses from this period acknowledged their mistakes in not having questioned the authority of the state and not having personally taken action. Some asserted that Germany is a country of law and order and that Germans of this generation typically followed the directives of those in power without opposing the most oppressive laws. For instance, many did not question the enforced practice of Jews wearing the Star of David armband, the prohibition of Germans from patronizing Jewish-owned businesses, or the routine house searches by the Gestapo for the removal and relocation of Jews. All of this was facilitated through the implementation of Nazi legislation, including the Nuremberg Laws, which ordinary Germans acquiesced to as mandated by the regime. This deference to authority and adherence to the law is deeply ingrained in German history, as evidenced in the literary works of numerous prominent German authors such as Heinrich von Kleist, Franz Kafka, and Heinrich Böll and warrants comprehensive research beyond the scope of this study.

As I did not personally live during the Nazi era, my understanding is derived solely from research and witness accounts. Although I have conducted hundreds of interviews, many of which were not published in this book, I did not personally experience this historical period. Consequently, it is essential to understand that our contemporary world is marked by global technology with innovations such as the Internet, mobile phones, WhatsApp, Instagram, and Facebook. In contrast, information during the Nazi era was conveyed by radio, at party rallies, and by word-of-mouth, all of which were closely monitored by the Nazi Party. Entire families were sent to concentration camps or sentenced to death for dissention, or for arbitrary reasons such as race, religion, sexuality, and political conviction. This is evident through the murder of six million Jews, and hundreds of thousands of Gypsies, communists, homosexuals, and regime opponents.

My intention in compiling this oral history was not to determine guilt or to seek answers to predefined questions, but rather to preserve the testimonies of those who lived during the Third Reich, allowing readers to draw their own conclusions. The work also functions as a treasure trove of recorded interviews to facilitate further academic research on this topic while preserving the actual voices of those who lived during this distressing and horrendous period in German history.

Acknowledgements

I would like to extend my sincere gratitude to several individuals for their invaluable contributions to this book. Their support, encouragement, and expertise have been instrumental in bringing this project to fruition.

First and foremost, I extend my deepest appreciation to my wife, Elisabeth, who recommended numerous interview partners during her work as a physiotherapist and gave me the opportunity to conduct the majority of these interviews. I would also like to thank my son, Nicholas, for his critical assessment of the book and suggestions for its improvement. Many thanks to my friend and fellow translator, Jürgen Schiffer, for his endless insistence that I complete this oral history after so many decades of work. I am also thankful to numerous friends and acquaintances whose recommendations opened the door and allowed me to speak with relatives who were in the war.

Finally, I am grateful to all my interview partners who took the time to share their life stories and had enough faith in me that I would write an honest depiction of their lives.

CHAPTER I

NATIONAL SOCIALISM

The Early Years and the Olympic Games

Anonymous woman was born in 1913 in Cologne. She recalls the early years of the Third Reich and the opening of the Olympic Games in 1936.

The politicians of the Weimar Republic lost the election, and Hitler was elected to office in 1933. And then I have to say that a time came when all the misery stopped – for whoever was willing to join the party. Whoever professed their loyalty to the Brownshirts – had it made. Since there were a large number of unemployed people – postal workers, railway workers, or anyone who was somehow unemployed – they simply went to them out of necessity because they were the only ones – how should I say it? – who promised them a future. We Germans are somehow romantic – and the ideas which Hitler presented in his speeches were like a bud that blossomed: "We will be someone again." I don't know whether that was only my own impression, but my father, who died in 1937, said: "Hitler is good, but all the little Hitlers [are the problem]." He said this in 1937.

And then there was something that I found to be very good back then and still think that it is good today. Hitler started to restructure everything from the bottom up. For example, young married couples didn't have enough money to start a household. They lacked basic things. And he then established the marriage loan. This meant that every young couple that wanted to get married and was willing to have children received a loan of one thousand Reichsmarks. Two hundred and fifty Reichsmarks were deducted from this amount for every child. If a woman gave birth to four children, the loan was paid off. He did things for the state and provided people with hope. And then people got married. Women were diligent and had children and were overworked. And then there was a convalescence programme, and the children were sent away to resorts. And, if necessary, mothers were allowed to visit resorts at least once a year – sometimes with their children, sometimes without children.

If they went without their children because they needed their rest, then girls from the League of German Girls or the Community Service helped out.

The German Young Folk was busy doing its duties while singing in uniform. An example was the year of compulsory community service. It was for all girls over 14 years of age. This meant that before you went out into the world, you had to do a year of practical work. You did this either in a family with children or on a farm or wherever it was necessary. In retrospect, I see this with great enthusiasm in comparison to the situation of the youth today. I don't have to tell you. You know what's going on. This is because of television, drugs, and the lack of time to raise children. In any case, I precisely remember that I was enthusiastic about these things. This began with the smallest children – I think that they were called "Pimpfen" – who were from 6 to 8 years of age – who had a small scarf and maybe a matching shirt – I don't know anymore – and a cap. And the entire group had a flag and sang and went to the woods and built fires. All of this was supervised by someone who was wearing a brown uniform, but was a youth. Whoever showed that they could work together with children gave the orders. They gathered wood together. It was pressure, but a pressure that they enjoyed together. They were small leaders. That's how it all began. Or, at least, this is how I remember it.

And the year of compulsory community service was difficult for the girls depending on where they were sent. I had one girlfriend – who has unfortunately died – who was the daughter of the director of the regional court. This meant that she came from a family with an academic background. She was sent to a family on a farm where there were a lot of children – I think five children – and a great deal of dirt. She later said when we were older: "That was the best time in my life." She would have been over-refined at home, but this year shaped her. The girls gained practical experience, had to show interest in sick people, and so on. And that's what's missing today. It became better and better. And then there was the Reich Labour Service for young people. It was the opposite of the work done by the BDM girls or the Community Service girls. They were in uniform. The Reich Labour Service had to be performed where there was work. Later, people said that Hitler only did that to get more children in order to go to war. That's what they said. That might be true.

But I saw that he did something in this period – and the Olympic Games were a part of it – for which foreign countries admired us. Until 1939 foreign countries couldn't say anything about the ideas that Hitler put into practice – until 1939 in Poland, 1940 in France. This led to what people see today as guilt, and which really is guilt. But this early history was so positive; it gave the Germans so much power and joy for the future that they became blind to the negative things which could be seen at that time.

For example, the Brownshirts gathered together and received their orders from their supervisors – whom we sarcastically called the "pheasants". They had khaki-brown uniforms just as the uniforms [of the police] are green and grey today. They had street fights and did bad things which they maybe didn't want to do, but they were forced to do. They had a profession and received wages, but belonged to a political party which called upon them to do this or that – forcing Jews to leave or other things. This was horrible, and it had a lasting effect on my mind. There were a lot of followers who did what the party wanted whether they wanted to or not. They had accepted the good part and now they had to do their duty. And if they didn't do it, then they themselves were fought. And if they did anything against it, then they were sent to the camps. But, at that time, we didn't know what was going on at the camps. I'll first tell you about this early period which included the Olympic Games.

These young girls not only worked during their year of compulsory community service, but they also became involved in sports clubs for gymnastics and different kinds of sports. And back then they wanted tall, blond, and healthy girls. I can still remember the field near Berlin. It was a huge field with young girls who were between 14 and 16 years old with white shirts and black shorts and who carried out their dancing exercises. It was so exact that you can hardly imagine. It was so inspiring. And the spectators in the stands were so enthusiastic. And Berlin was full of people from outside of the city. You couldn't even find the smallest room in Berlin. You really had to be lucky. And we were lucky. I travelled to Berlin together with my sister and her husband because we were able to stay in the flat of people who were abroad or something. In Berlin, there were large flats with five to seven rooms with an entrance for the servants and another for the owner. And we were able to stay in such a flat during the Olympic Games. It was difficult to get tickets – very difficult to get tickets. My brother-in-law got us the tickets and the flat. Unfortunately, I didn't see much of the Games. After three days I left the city because I had a son who was about 1 year old, and I was worried about whether he was well taken care of. Back then there weren't televisions like today. It started at that time. People got together wherever there was a television and watched the Games. Television and radio were part of this period. It was unbelievable even from today's perspective.

The Church in the Third Reich

Pastor's wife wishes to remain anonymous. Her husband was the pastor at a Protestant church in a small village in Sauerland (North Rhine-Westphalia) where he faced great opposition from the SA and the German Christians during the Nazi regime.

During World War II, it was very difficult here in the parish because National Socialism also attacked the Church. You weren't able to be part of their world view. In any case, my husband recognized this from the very beginning. The people were so enthusiastic here, and he couldn't go along with it because he understood the background, and he knew what would become of this world view, and this actually happened. And the worst was in 1934. In the parish it reached a critical point, and we were sharply attacked – most people didn't go to church services anymore – didn't say hello to us anymore, and we were extremely isolated. While the SA was marching through the streets, we were creeping behind windows in order not to be seen. Beware if you didn't greet others with a raised arm – then you were reported to the authorities.[1]

That was here in Breckerfeld?

That was here in this small village. And we weren't in a large city. And then it was really bad here in 1934. In the neighbouring parish – it was a very small parish on the main road – there was a German Christian.[2] He was an acquaintance of my husband – he had studied with him earlier. And my husband was forbidden from preaching, and he also wasn't allowed to leave the house on Sunday mornings. Behind the parish house there was a large sports field. The SA gathered there – people from here and from the other parish – and the pastor from the German Christians held church services on the field. Don't ask me how.

I went to our church and it was full. Of course, we had people on our side – when it came down to professing their faith they were there – especially people from our group. I went to the church service although there was no pastor – my husband was at home and wasn't allowed to leave the house. And then a presbyter came, or rather it was a church elder, and he led us in songs and prayer, and we went back home. And that's the way it was sometimes. There was so much hatred towards the pastor and that was so sad. We were well liked and respected in the parish, but then the hatred became too much – the political hatred. We had a great deal of fear – a great deal of fear.

Was there an opportunity to oppose the party?

Yes. Everyone knew the other's position. For example, on Reformation Day, my husband was preaching and followed the instructions of the Confessing Church precisely.[3] And he always read out loud the list of pastors who had been arrested and so on. And that was forbidden. That was forbidden. But my husband always read it out loud – always – always. And the police were in the church and they had to write that down. But we had a police officer here in our parish who was friendly towards us. And he came to the parish house on Monday morning, went into the study, and said to my husband: "What should I write?" He was a very decent man. He left out the most dangerous things. And, of course, that helped us quite a bit. But this man – he was a so-called "old fighter" – he was a member of the party before 1933 – at the end of the war when all the people had to be "denazified" – that's what they called it – they needed someone to vouch for them – and then they all came running to the parish house – the civil servants, the teachers, all the people who were a part of it – and then my husband had to answer questions: "Were they dangerous back then? Or not? Or were they harmless?" He knew all of them – I remember that so clearly today – none of those people who think differently today can fool me. But he helped people as much as he could – that is clear – that is clear – some of them were harmless people who were instigated – but we also experienced horrible things.

On this Reformation Day, he held a powerful sermon in the morning and voiced his opinion – and the parish here was very large, and he visited many sick people. And in the afternoon – it was at the end of October – on

Reformation Day – he visited parish members in the country and came home totally soaked. He never had the habit of taking off his shoes and walking around the house in slippers. And on that day – he was so wet – he took off his shoes at home – it was already dark – and then suddenly we heard a group of men singing a song outside: "A Mighty Fortress is our God". My husband thought that those were people on his side who wanted to support him in some sort of way. He opened the window, and we were bombarded with a barrage of obscenities – and they were swearing at him – it was eerie. And who were these people? The entire SA – the entire SA – all the men here had to obey – our friends were there, the principal from the high school – by the way, he never returned home from the war – they all had to pay a high price. We had a reading circle together with them and met them every week – and all of them were there and joined in. It was a horribly rainy day and dark, and I was terribly afraid – I was expecting my second child – and I didn't know what would happen. And then I was afraid that my husband would run out the front door, and fortunately he had his slippers on so that he couldn't run out immediately – he wasn't afraid at all. And then the doorbell rang, and it was the Christian youth who were on our side – and they wanted to come into our house – for our protection – young men – for example, there were our neighbours, and they were all there. Of course, that was really nice for us. And then my husband didn't go outside. They said to him: "Don't go outside, Pastor. The police are there, and they'll arrest you immediately." And then they went away. And on the following morning, we saw how they had destroyed our yard. The hatred was so great – the hatred for people who thought differently. All the men had to join the SA otherwise they lost their jobs – there were a lot of them who didn't think that way from the bottom of their hearts – but they couldn't do anything about it.

These were people from the parish who went to church every week?

Yes. Certainly. They were also there. And friends. Everyone. This high school principal came to our house a few days later – I was there – and he wanted to convince my husband to change his way of thinking and become a German Christian. Yes, that's what he said – and then I saw my husband open up the door – that was his friend – and he said that he couldn't see eye to eye with him anymore and that he had to go. And this man – he was drafted into the war and paid with his life.

What did they demand from your husband?

He was supposed to follow the party line – he was supposed to become a National Socialist – he was supposed to join them. Their ideology was completely different. There were German Christians – for example, there was a pastor in Hagen who took down the crucifix from the altar and hung up a picture of Hitler. This was the cult. Hitler was worshipped. Hitler was their God. That's the way it was.

Hitler Youth

Heinz Kendziora was born in Lusatia (Brandenburg) in 1923. He recalls his childhood in the Third Reich.

When Hitler came to power in 1933, my father spoke negatively about him because my father supported the SPD [Social Democratic Party]. He didn't want to have anything to do with Hitler. For that reason, I had to wait a long time before I was able to join the German Young Folk and the Hitler Youth. When you were at school you went to the German Young Folk and afterwards to the Hitler Youth.[4] All my friends had already joined and told me about the fun things they were doing such as travelling and sleeping over somewhere. I thought it was really adventurous. But I wasn't allowed to – until my father decided to become affiliated with the [Nazi] Party in 1935. He voluntarily joined the SA – and then I was able to join the Hitler Youth. There was a tendency back then to think that who was not for the party was against it. And he probably thought that it was better to associate with the National Socialists to advance his career – although he never formally joined the party. That's how I would express it.

I first went to the German Young Folk – boys up to 14 years of age called "Pimpfen" who were still in school. The 15-and-16-year-olds then went through an apprenticeship in the Hitler Youth – which was abbreviated HJ. These boys basically did the same things as the German Young Folk, but more extensively and directed towards pre-military training – field exercises and everything that was later needed in war. I wouldn't say that it was a preparation for war – at least we didn't see it that way. It was presented in such a crafty way, and young people are very susceptible to adventurous things: camping, campfires, and things that never existed before. And it really interested me. I would say that it was comparable to the Boy Scouts today. Afterwards there was military training for the war – I can't remember what it was called anymore – with boys from the Hitler Youth involved in military drills. And I believe they were called up for military service beginning at the age of 16. During the training, we had to learn everything about our greatly beloved Führer: his birthday and life story. All the National Socialist holidays had to be learned by heart. We were – how should I say it – greatly impressed by National Socialism. I thought: “It’s a good thing.” My father received work again – although times were hard back then. There was high unemployment, and he got a job. I thought: “Wonderful.” That was our first impression. And that’s how they continued to bring us up. Once you were part of it – and almost everyone was – they wouldn’t let go of you anymore. They shaped you the way they wanted to. Goebbels managed to get everything the way he wanted. You have to say that he was an intelligent man – although he had his dark side.

With this background in mind, I started talking to others my own age who were being drafted. Many of them had joined voluntarily. So, I said to my friend: “You know what? Let’s join, too.” We joined voluntarily in 1940 or 1941, but because of my job – work that was important for the war effort – I didn’t have to go to Reich Labour Service. I was exempted. But since I had joined voluntarily – they would have drafted me anyway because I was 18 – the navy called me up for military service.

Willi Schuster was born in Mönchengladbach in 1923. He recalls his experiences in the Hitler Youth.

When I was 10 years old in 1933, we had the German Young Folk [Deutsches Jungvolk] here in Germany. That was an organization founded by Adolf Hitler. Nobody knew it beforehand. And we joined because it was fun. It wasn’t for political reasons, but rather to be together with other children and to play cops and robbers or similar games in the woods and fields. There were also evening meetings which I didn’t enjoy. They talked about and taught political topics which didn’t interest me at all as a 10-year-old boy. We were asked questions about the leadership in the National Socialist Party and such things. Later when I was 14 years old, I went to the Aviator Hitler Youth because I enjoyed model airplanes – we built model airplanes there. We also learned about gliders in Nöthen in the Eifel Mountains, and I also learned Morse code – the radio operator's alphabet. It was an incentive for me when I was older – I thought that if I had to be a soldier, then I wanted to go to the air force – to be part of the flight staff. I had difficulties achieving that because I wore glasses and that meant that you normally weren't allowed to fly an airplane. The regulations were relaxed somewhat during the war – I was allowed to become a radio operator. I enjoyed learning Morse code. I volunteered for the air force so that they wouldn't draft me and send me somewhere I didn't want to go. I didn't go to the army, but to the air force as a volunteer during the war. I went to school and was trained to become a radio operator in 1942. I received my high school diploma in 1942, and a few days after graduation I became a soldier.

Visits by Hitler

Dieter Behringer was born in Coburg (Upper Franconia) in 1926. His father joined the National Socialist Party in 1925 and was an acquaintance of Hitler and Göring. During the war, his father's factory was converted into an armaments plant for the production of anti-tank mines. Behringer talks about his childhood memories.

My father was almost a co-founder of the National Socialist Party. He joined the party in 1925.

That's extremely early.

Yes. He received the Golden Party Badge.[5] It was very early.

How did that come about? Was he a personal friend of Hitler's?

No. They were acquaintances. Just like the two of us.

Did he regret it in later years? Or what was his position?

His position was – how should I express it? – he explicitly stated that Hitler's entire manner had a strong influence on him – and that Hitler didn't remain the same person that he was when my father joined the party. The later Hitler had nothing in common with this earlier person. My father also knew Göring – he knew the whole government – except for a few individuals such as Rosenberg.[6] He didn't want to have anything to do with those people. And then later with Bormann[7] – because he also openly said: "That's not a man for us. He's in the wrong position." And those were the worst guys. It may sound very far-fetched, but my father didn't know the least about the concentration camps – and I would stake my life on it.

Did you ever see any of these prominent people at your house?

Yes. Certainly. I knew Hitler.

Really? He came to visit?

Yes. Not regularly. If he was in Coburg, then my father met with him. My father had only one eye – he was blinded in one eye as a child – and that's why he always took me along with him.

How would you describe Hitler?

Well, how was he? You could talk to him just as easily as we're talking now. He wasn't a braggart in any sort of way. That was the strange thing about him.

You could talk with him?

Yes. You could talk with him.

And you didn't suspect anything?

No. You didn't suspect that so much maliciousness was inside of him. You really couldn't imagine that.

Were other prominent people also at your house?

No. No. Göring kept his distance from all private contact. That's what I always noticed as a child and a young boy. Who else was there? – What was his name? – Speer – the so-called "architect".[8]

How old were you when they came to your house?

That was in the beginning. Afterwards, during the war they didn't come anymore. When was that? Maybe in 1936. 1937. 1938. Somewhere around that time. I was 10 years old, but I noticed everything.

Sudetenland (October 1938)

Walter Scharnagl was born in Plan near Marienbad in Czechoslovakia. He recalls the annexation of the Sudetenland in October 1938 following the Munich Agreement.

In our school there were some students who were really German nationalists. Certain things took place at our school. We were a strictly German town. There were hardly – hardly any Czechs – a few – there wasn't much contact with Czech families. I remember – I believe that it was on 7 March – there was always a holiday, Memorial Day – it was the birthday of the already deceased first Czech president Masaryk. And they always commemorated him at school. There was a celebration in the assembly hall, and the Czech national anthem was always sung: "Where is my home?" [Kde domov můj?] Some of the German nationalists – we were 14 years old at that time – some of the graduating students – who were politically active – started singing the German national anthem instead of the Czech national anthem as a demonstration and protest. It was a big circus.

Or another time in the spring of 1939, I went to school early in the morning with my neighbour, a schoolmate of mine, and we were stopped on the street by upper classmates from our school. "There's no school today. There's a school strike today. We're on strike against the police." And we had to go back home again. Of course, there were always investigations. The Czech national police came and interrogated people: "Who was it? Who organized it?" It was always very colourful. Or there was the market square. In the late afternoon or early evening there was always the so-called "stroll". People strolled along – they went for a walk – on the large market square that you often find in the East. The boys and girls walked on the sidewalk. And then they strolled as a kind of demonstration, meaning that they walked with one foot up on the sidewalk and the other foot below in the street just to aggravate the police. They did this one after the other in a row. Demonstrations were forbidden, but no one could say anything. They were taking a walk, but very strangely. These were demonstrations resulting from the political tension.

Elisabeth Bost was born in 1924 in Chomutov in the Sudetenland. She recalls the annexation of Czechoslovakia by the Nazis in 1938.

During the political negotiations everyone hoped for an agreement with Germany because we had a very difficult political and economic situation [in Czechoslovakia]. We had high unemployment – of course especially among the Germans. We had a teacher training school and an engineering school in town – all of these students hardly had any job prospects because Czechs were given jobs first everywhere. Germans were discriminated against before 1938. As everywhere else in the world, minorities are not well liked. Approximately six million Czechs lived in Czechoslovakia, almost four million Germans, and then Slovaks, Hungarians, and also a few Poles, but they weren't crucial. It was a multi-ethnic country about which promises were made by the Czechs in 1918. It was supposed to be similar to Switzerland. But those promises were never held. And that is what made people so furious. Everyone was so happy when they heard about the annexation to Germany. My father was on the market square when German troops marched into Chomutov. He started a conversation with German officers who told him that the annexation of the Sudetenland was not the end. It was going to continue and there was going to be war. My father returned home terribly distraught. He had experienced World War I as a young man, and war was something horrible for him.

What happened after the annexation of Czechoslovakia?

The Czechs who lived in Chomutov – voluntarily – left for the interior of Bohemia – which was later called the "Protectorate", established in the spring. But some of them remained – my father knew some Czechs.

We had a good relationship with the Czechs who had been in the border area for a long time. Multi-ethnic groups often understand one another well – it's the politicians who bring about the disharmony. I don't know of any reasons why the Czechs should have been afraid – they weren't taken prisoner or mistreated. I don't know of anything like that.

What did you do during this time?

I was still at school. My father worked at the teacher training centre and was responsible for supervising the library. And then the first difficulties arose: in Germany, the literary works of Tucholsky, and Jews in general, or Thomas Mann were all burned. And this literature had to be removed from the library in the teacher training centre. My father was distraught – he said: "I had to give away far too many books." We lived together with my grandparents in a large house. My grandfather's name was Levi, and we had difficulty getting our family ancestry book.[9] Great difficulty. My brother died in 1941. My father's status as a civil servant wasn't extended. He was removed from the teacher training centre and transferred to a high school in Leitmeritz. And he had extreme difficulties there. In the teacher training centre, there were students who were seriously preparing for teaching jobs, and in the high school in Leitmeritz he wasn't able to establish any discipline. The Hitler Youth was very strong, and he had great difficulties. After my brother had died, my father also died shortly afterwards: In November my brother passed away, and in September the following year my father. Three days later, my mother was awarded the Honorary Aryan Award from Berlin. We had no idea what had conspired behind the scenes.

How were lessons at school after the annexation?

There were teachers at school who were very objective and continued the old lessons. But we had a German teacher – who had a very Czech name – and he was a fanatical National Socialist – absolutely anti-clerical. Teachers like this also existed. The subjects themselves didn't change at school, only the content. Latin and Mathematics remained the same. But, in German and History, other topics were given precedence such as the history of the German Empire. And in Biology there was the topic of "blood and soil" and the mythology of the twentieth century. Whenever Hitler held a speech, we were called together. We came into a large hall and listened to Hitler's speech. The boys at school were in the Hitler Youth and the girls in the League of German Girls – it didn't appeal to me. But they were involved in sporting activities, and games were played together. All of this was shaped by National Socialist ideology and by slogans such as "blood and soil" and "Nordic" and so on. This was extremely intense. There were also young teachers who viewed all of this critically – but afterwards they were called up for military service. Our English teacher fell in battle. They all later became soldiers. Then the old teachers returned, and lessons were very calm and moderate. That took place until graduation. Our fellow students left the school at the age of 16 [to work] as anti-aircraft helpers. It was wartime. They took so-called "emergency exams". And the remaining students – eight other girls and the two boys – who were ill – and couldn't be drafted – the eleven of us – took the final high school examination in 1943.

Night of Broken Glass (November 1938)

Willi Bartmann was born in Wuppertal in North Rhine-Westphalia in 1921. He recalls the day after the Night of Broken Glass in his high school.

We had five Jews in our school, and four of them were in our class. And then there were four Catholics. And a lot of boys were sons of Protestant pastors and missionaries. Wuppertal is well known for pious Protestants, and the Rhine Missionary Society is still in Wuppertal today. They were all nice boys, and our Jewish schoolmates were also nice. We got along well together. I had to join the Hitler Youth so that my father would get the tuition money reimbursed because I still lived at home. We were able to take care of that cleverly. I went to the Hitler Youth Navy in Wuppertal – the "Pirates". The Wupper River had eight centimetres of water back then and it was also dirty. So, you couldn't do a lot with it. But I had to present my Hitler Youth card every year – with a few blue stamps attached to it – to show that I had actually been there. They never checked. The city was simply too big, or maybe the people there were more lenient. I know that it was much worse in other places. But we got the money regularly. When I went to this school, they didn't put me in the right grade. They couldn't because I was one or two years older than the other pupils. There were some advantages for me because certain things were easier to learn. I was in school until 1940 – until they drafted me as a soldier in February 1940.

You mentioned that there were a few Jewish guys in your class. What happened on 10 November 1938?

Basically, there is nothing to tell because nothing really happened back then. I don't mind telling their names. Balheimer – he was a nice boy, but such a carefree cheerful guy. It was just unbelievable. You just had to love him. Balheimer left our class because he had to repeat the grade. Aaron, Grünewald, Ostwald – that was the alphabetical order that I still remember today. Aaron was the leader of the Jewish pupils. He could trace his family tree back to Aaron and Moses – they were Sephardic Jews from Spain. And the others – I wouldn't say that they bowed to him – but he was the most respected. Besides, he was a big heavy guy. I once met his father. He was a lawyer or something like that at the local court or regional court. He was a big strong man over two metres tall. He looked like Ibn Saud, who was also a big heavy guy with a hook nose – if you remember him?[10] I can't say anything bad about these three boys at all. Grünewald was our Greek scholar. He took the Greek lessons extremely seriously. And ten of us would stand around his desk before the lessons began. "Grüni, what does this mean here? What is this? What is this? And what's that?"

And now to 10 November 1938.[11] The three Jewish boys were in school on the following day. They had slept poorly during the night. But nothing had happened to them. They talked about it, though. Jews were assaulted throughout the entire city. A piano and a bed were thrown out a window in their homes and some windows were smashed. But nothing happened to these three boys. The school normally started at 8:10 am because some pupils came from far-away places like Barmen, Solingen, and one came from Hagen. That's why it didn't begin at 8:00 am, but rather at 8:10 am. And our Greek teacher didn't arrive at 8:10 am. He also wasn't there at 8:15 am. He first arrived at 8:30 am. The classroom was extremely loud. We had been talking with the three Jewish boys. We didn't suspect anything. And then Dr Egon Kirchner came in. His face was deathly pale. He was holding a piece of paper in his hand. And for once he didn't say: "Heil Hitler!" He used to lift his hand to his waist and say "Heil Hitler!" just because he had to. And on this morning, he didn't say it. Instead, he told everyone to listen up. There was a decree from the Reich's cultural minister – or whatever he was called – the Prussian cultural minister. It was from the previous day, but it was so important that it had already arrived. Normally it took fourteen days or three weeks. "Effective immediately Jews have to leave German schools", he stated. What else was he supposed to say? It was effective immediately. "You can say your goodbyes."

What happened?

Everyone cried. Everyone cried. And, of course, our three Jewish schoolmates cried the most. We said our goodbyes. We asked them what they were going to do now. Of course, they knew what was going on. And Ostwald and Aaron went to South America. It was clear back then that they couldn't stay – that was understandable. But for Grünewald it was somewhat different. He said: "No. No. My father wants to stay here. He served in World War I and was wounded. The Nazis won't do anything to us." In any case, they left the school crying within ten minutes. We sat there really dumbfounded. I was a few years older than the others, but I was just as dumbfounded. And then we had the second lesson – which was also Greek – from Dr Egon Kirchner. He was a senior teacher from Kötzschenbroda. That's in Saxony. He spoke a little Saxon like this. [He imitates his Saxon pronunciation.] We always used to laugh. And then he told us about the persecution of the Jews and stories of Judith and Esther and Holofernes. I thought to myself: "Is this guy crazy?" He was a presbyter in the Protestant church, was well versed in the Bible, participated in the congregation, and told us about the persecution of the Jews in the Old Testament. We sat there, and we couldn't believe it. And his face changed from red to white. The man must have suffered terribly. And then he went out after the bell rang for the long break. And, again, he didn't say "Heil Hitler!" And we sat there and thought: "What's happening now? What's happening now? What's happening now?" In any case, our Jewish schoolmates were gone. And the war came after that. In that same year, Ostwald and Aaron actually went to South America. They sold everything – probably as fast as they could. They probably gave away a lot. I don't know. They didn't have much money.

After 10 November 1938 we didn't hear anything anymore from our two Jewish schoolmates, Ostwald and Aaron. And after the war we found out by chance what had happened to Grünewald. I had already known my wife back then, and we would always go for walks in the woods in the evenings and would see a nice middle-aged woman. We started a conversation, and she told us that she was half Jewish and that the Nazis had removed her spleen to see how well someone could live without a spleen. At that time, she was suing Prussia or the Reich. I can't tell you the details because we lost contact with one another. And then I asked her about Grünewald, the last Jewish boy. And she said that the Grünewalds were left pretty much alone until 1942. But then in 1942, the grandmother and grandfather, the mother and father, Grünewald, who was in our class, and his sister were sent to Theresienstadt. And they were all gassed.

Marie-Augusta Heibel was born in 1918 in Bergisch Gladbach near Cologne. In 1938 she travelled to Berlin to visit her brother, who was suffering from the flu in a military hospital. On the morning of 10 November, she left her hotel to discover the devastation that the Nazis had left from the previous night.

At the time of the infamous Night of Broken Glass, when the synagogues were burned and Jewish shops destroyed, I was with my brother in Berlin. He was in the cavalry. His regiment was in the vicinity of Berlin, and he caught a bad flu and had to go to Berlin to a military hospital. And I travelled there to visit him. One morning in front of my hotel on the way to the military hospital, I thought to myself: "What is that?" There was smoke. Something was burning, or rather it was smouldering more than burning. And then I said to someone: "For Heaven's sake, what happened here?" A young man in uniform looked at me and said: "The synagogue is burning." "Why is it burning?" I asked. "They started it on fire last night. Don't you remember?" he said. "I was sleeping last night. How should I know that? And why?" I asked. He didn't know either. Well, then I went to the military hospital, and they had heard about it in the meantime. They said that the Nazis had set the synagogues on fire – but they didn't know any more than that. The next day I travelled to Berlin to meet my aunt. Kurfürstendamm, [the main avenue in Berlin], looked bad – really – every second shop, or at least every third shop was destroyed – in other words: Jewish shops. I had no idea that there were so many Jewish shops there.

And then when I returned home – I only stayed there until my brother was discharged – his two-year service was over – we travelled home together – and my father told us the following story. Hohe Street in Cologne is not as beautiful as the Königsallee in Düsseldorf, but it used to be just as elegant. In any case, there was a weapons shop in Hohe Street where you could buy hunting weapons – my father was a passionate hunter – he wasn't someone who shot at everything that moved, but rather he made sure that he had good bucks on his hunting grounds that bred. Well, over the years he had bought everything that he needed for hunting in this shop. And Mr Kettner – he was the owner of the shop – lived above his shop in the same building just one floor higher. He was awakened during the night by a terrible clattering and screaming and so on – went to the window and looked outside and saw how – across the street there was a shoe store – a big shoe store – everyone certainly knew that they were Jews, but it didn't interest us – I always went there when I bought shoes – and he saw how civilians were pulling everything from the shop and throwing it onto the street – the shoes and everything. And Mr Kettner picked up the phone and called the police and said that they should come quickly because people were looting a shop. Do you know what the police told him? "Mr Kettner, don't worry – just go back to bed. Everything's all right. Nothing will happen to you." And afterwards people found out who these civilians were – they were the SA – who normally wore brown uniforms – and so that they wouldn't be recognized they first of all dressed in plain clothes – and secondly the SA from Düsseldorf did this in Cologne and the SA from Cologne did this in Düsseldorf.

Cilli Gottfeld was born in Stettin in Pomerania in 1921 to Jewish parents. The family jewellery shop was vandalized on the Night of Broken Glass and her father was held in a concentration camp for three months. In August 1939, the family fled from Germany to Shanghai, China.

We had affidavits for America, but we didn't have any time left. My father had seven brothers – five of them were alive – one of them went to Chile – and all the others, who were on the Front in World War I, stupidly said that nothing bad would happen to us. And I had an aunt –

my mother's sister – she was a very young widow and a strong-willed person – she said that we had to go. It didn't matter where – we had to leave Germany. It would get worse. As it turned out, you couldn't leave the country a month later. So, we left on a Japanese steamer which took four weeks. We arrived in China on a terribly hot day on 1 August. The war started on 1 September. That was one month before the start of the war. And we were still able to take along two big containers. But we had to pay the government for our own furniture and everything. At least we were able to take these things along. And, of course, what we did – my father was a jeweller – we hid things everywhere – you know – to help ourselves – big bronze statues and things like that and many carpets – expensive carpets – and we hid jewels in lard and sausages. We told them that we needed these things. They asked us why we needed these things, and we told them that it reminded us of home. In any case, we arrived there on a very hot day, and I liked it from the very beginning because I didn't have to be afraid to go through the streets – everyone was kind. The Chinese were kind in any case – I don't know how they are to foreigners today, but at that time they were kind and friendly – and as a child [in Germany] I was afraid to say something wrong in the cinema or anywhere. You were afraid to open your mouth, but there [in Shanghai] you could say anything and walk through the streets and you were free.

Willi Schuster was born in Mönchengladbach in 1923. He remembers the Night of Broken Glass as a 15-year-old boy in Bad Godesberg near Bonn.

I was playing football with other schoolmates on the street. And then suddenly one of the kids came on his bicycle and said: "Something's burning in the city. There's a fire." We stopped playing football, got onto our bikes, and rode there to see where it was burning. It was something special if something was burning. 1938 was a time of peace – there was no war. And I rode my bike to the city and saw that on the corner across from Aenchen [restaurant] there was a smouldering fire. It wasn't a blazing fire, but smoke rose into the air. And a building was burning there. The men from the fire brigade were standing around and didn't do anything. And as a 15-year-old boy I said: "Where's the water? I'll put the fire out." And then they said: "Young boy, stay back. We have it under control. We have it under control." And then I watched, and the fire burned down – it was a synagogue. And then I rode my bike up Burg Street, and there were several Jewish stores with smashed windows. I didn't understand what was going on. I didn't know why it happened. [weeps] I saw this, and naturally I heard that there was a worldwide Jewry that was our sworn enemy. This is what the National Socialists said back then. They said that the Jews were the enemy of Germany and the German people. They were dangerous and had to be fought.

Helene Baake was born in Adendorf near Bonn in 1924. She worked as an apprentice in a shop on the day following the Night of Broken Glass.

I was working in a shop as an apprentice, and apprentices had to go to the customers in the morning with a sheet of paper and write down what they wanted delivered. On another street there was a house where Specht is today – first there was Schmitz Bakery, then a shoe store, and then a courtyard where the sexton lived, and next to the sexton was Specht. And he had a driveway leading to the back. And inside the building was a carpenter's shop – and those were Jews. I didn't know that at the time. And on that day – after the night in which they destroyed shops and shot at and killed Jews – I brought a basket to the Jews. My boss said to me: "I can't go there. You have to go there. Nobody knows you here." And then I brought them a large basket of goods. And we never heard anything from those people again.

How did your boss know that something was wrong?

I don't know how he knew it. He never spoke about it, and, honestly, I never asked about it.

Elisabeth Neff was born in Stolp (Eastern Pomerania) in 1923. She recalls the Night of Broken Glass as a 15-year-old girl.

1938 arrived. My father knew some Jews. But I believe that there were very few Jews. However, my father always said that he preferred to go to the Jews because he could bargain with them when he bought something. But I didn't need to buy anything. My parents bought everything. And there were banners: "Don't Buy from Jews". But I never knew who the Jews were until 1938 after the so-called "Night of Broken Glass". Suddenly, a great number of businesses were destroyed. I had never imaged that they were Jews. A wonderful, very beautiful delicatessen shop – Bröske – was destroyed. It was located right when you walked through the New Gate of the city – it was a large building where hotel owners went to shop for the most expensive things. It was a very beautiful store – a delicatessen. And on the market square there were three or four or five shops that had been destroyed. And then I was told that I should go to the synagogue. I went there and saw that it was burning and that no one was extinguishing the fire. And I went home crying and said: "They're crazy!" That was everything. No one at home talked about it. And I don't know any more than that. I thought that it was unbelievable.

Hedwig Salz was born in Bonn-Dottendorf in 1932. She remembers the Night of Broken Glass as a six-year-old girl.

We had a family shop and sold milk among other things. My father delivered milk in the mornings, and I went along with him. I wasn't in school yet. We were standing around the truck while the milk was being delivered, and the customers were there. I remember the horribly oppressive atmosphere. I didn't know exactly what had happened, but I knew that it was horrible, and that we weren't allowed to talk about it out loud. I noticed that something had happened to the Jews during the night in Bonn. That's my recollection of the Night of Broken Glass.

Did you witness anything?

Not personally. But we had customers in our shop – Jews – and they weren't allowed to enter the shop when other people were there. My mother somehow arranged with them to come during the afternoon break when the shop was closed. They had a furniture store in Bonn – Leopold – and lived in our neighbourhood in Dottendorf. And Mr David – if I remember his name correctly – was a Jew – he didn't leave back then – although he could have as he told us. He didn't leave because his wife was ill and received treatment at the heart centre in Bonn-Endenich. I don't remember anymore which illness she had – but she went there. They came to our shop as long as possible. Afterwards, we never saw them again.

What kind of shop did your parents have?

Groceries: milk, butter, eggs, cheese, and later, larger articles. We were basically limited to Dottendorf. That's how my parents survived. Officially no one spoke about what had happened to the Jews. I remember that during the war people had to stand in long lines. Lots of people waited and talked. Once someone from the Nazi Party came to our shop and asked: "You hear a lot of things. Do you know who is talking about what?" My mother then answered: "I'm so busy. I don't hear anything." We knew that there were people with such big ears who passed on information.

Josef Salz was born in Neustadt (Wied) in Westerwald in 1927. He remembers the Night of Broken Glass from his childhood.

We had farmland, and cattle traders came to us regularly – those were Jews from Rheinbreitbach. It was always nice when they came because they had a car and took us children along. It was a real experience back then. There were hardly any cars. And at some point – they were gone. They emigrated and that's all we heard of them. Other cattle traders came, and my father said: “I liked the Jews better. These others are much more calculating.” I know that there were political problems back then. On the Night of Broken Glass, a doctor’s surgery in Linz was destroyed – it was a doctor who was well known for his charitable work to families who couldn’t pay. We found it so unfair that they did that to the man who really had a good reputation. The remaining trust that we had in the party was then gone.

Deportation of the Jews

Hannelore Füssenich was born in Cologne in 1923. She remembers the deportation of Jews from Cologne.

I had many Jewish girlfriends in Cologne. I lived directly on Neumarkt, and there were a great number of Jewish stores. And there were Jewish children that I used to play with. I saw how they were simply taken from their homes. For example, there were two sisters who were taken from their homes. I saw it and ran after them. "Where are you going? Where are you going?" I shouted. That was my first confrontation with the deportation of Jews. And they were sent to concentration camps, but no one even knew about the concentration camps. Today it is sometimes presented as if everyone knew. But people didn't know. That came much later. Much later.

Did you often witness Jews being deported?

Yes, of course, I did. I saw it a few times. For example, on Garrison Street there was a very wealthy couple who were jewellers. They were also taken away. Auerbach was their name. A very good friend of mine by the name of Röschen lived in Lungengasse – and those were rich Jews – and they always collected me from home on their bikes. They were very Orthodox Jews. I always carried the menorah into the dining room for them. They didn't touch or use the doorbell. And I always got matzo as a present. [laughs] They recognized what was going on and left for Jerusalem before it started with the Jews.

What did the neighbours say?

They were shaken. They were horrified. You didn't see hatred of the Jews. On the contrary. We were powerless because the Gestapo came. And, of course, we were afraid. We were afraid of the Gestapo. You only saw the Gestapo when they picked up Jews. They came in cars and were almost always dressed in black leather coats or leather jackets – or trench coats. The Gestapo Headquarters in Cologne was on Appellhofplatz. It was called the EL-DE House.[12]

Annelies Spiller was born in Katowice in present-day Poland in 1923. She recalls the deportation of a Jewish family in 1938/39 and the acquiescent response of her family and neighbours.

A Jewish family lived across the street from us when we moved into our house in 1938. I noticed the girls immediately because they had wonderfully beautiful red hair. And one day – it must have been at the beginning of 1939 or end of 1938 – the windows were suddenly bare and the curtains gone. And then I said to my mother: "Mom, did you notice? The people across the street seemed to have moved. Where did they go?" My mother thought for a moment and then said to me: "Well, they recently wrote that Jewish families were supposed to be relocated." And the matter was settled. I didn't say anything. And that's what young people could hold against my generation today. We didn't ask questions. You know? We didn't ask questions. A few days later a young man moved into the house with his mother, and he interested me more than the people who used to live there. You know? We simply didn't ask questions. We accepted it – not maliciously – but rather because we thought that they simply were gone. We simply accepted the fact that they had been relocated. When I came to my new school in 1937, I knew that there was a Jewish girl there. And she went to South America with her parents. You know? We heard about it. But we never asked why and for what reason. "What did they do to you? Or what happened to your father? How are you getting there?" We simply didn't ask. The major fault of my generation was that we simply accepted what we were told. We didn't do it maliciously, but rather we trusted the government and thought that everything would be alright. The government would do the right thing. They couldn't possible do wrong. And now we have the consequences.

Wilhelm Blatzheim was born in Bad Godesberg near Bonn in 1926. He remembers a Jewish family from his neighbourhood.

My parents had a shop in Bad Godesberg – with a large hairdressing salon – where many customers were Jewish women from the area – some wives of butchers and others of weavers and so on. They were very simple people like everyone else, and I never had the feeling that they were different from us – until one day we were told that we had to be careful. I remember – and my mother told me the story – that two Jewish women came to us late one evening to have their hair done because it was forbidden during the day. My mother was then given money – I don't know from whom – and instructed not to serve Jews anymore. I personally saw that across the street from my parents' house in Friesdorferstraße there were one or two men in the entrance of the building who observed our house day and night. On the day before [the Jewish family] was deported – which we ourselves did not see – Mrs Oster, who lived about 50 metres away from my parents' house, gave my mother four small crystal vases and bowls. That was everything they had left because they were forced to sell everything in order to buy groceries. And my wife still has these items today upstairs. The small bowls weren't worth much. The family didn't have any money, but gave them to my mother as a memento. They said to my mother: "We want to say goodbye to the Blatzheims. We probably won't see you again." And that was the last time we heard from them. We never heard anything again.

Wolfgang Heine was born in Berlin in 1925. He remembers Jewish neighbours in Berlin-Steglitz during his childhood years.

Across from our home in Steglitz there was a building of flats with six families. It was very interesting. On the Night of Broken Glass – Jewish shops were destroyed – and later, Jews had to wear the yellow star. Until 1938 everything took its course, but then National Socialism showed its hideous face. Now I'll tell you about the building of flats across the street. A man by the name of Klut lived on the top left floor. He was the recipient of the Blood Order – one of the men who was in the Beer Hall Putsch on 9 November [1923].[13] He had been [in Munich] back then and had been injured and also received the Golden Party Badge. He was a very staunch Nazi. The man on the top right had an automotive garage, and below him was a high-level civil servant, and on the bottom right was an active SS lieutenant colonel [SS Obersturmbannführer].

And below Klut – this major Nazi – there was the family Neustädter. And they were Jews. In our neighbourhood there were the Neustädters, the Rosenbergers, and so on. All of them Jews. I would say that in every building of flats – or in every second building – there was a Jew. Everyone lived together peacefully. There were never any problems. It only became known afterwards that he was Jewish. We didn't know at all. But it didn't matter to us. Mr Neustädter was one of the leading engineers at Siemens and had – I believe – around fifty patents for electricity insulation, above-ground installations, high-tension wires, and so on. Until the beginning of 1943 – during the war – Mr Neustädter was collected every morning by a Siemens company car with a chauffeur. Behind this car was an SS vehicle for the Obersturmbannführer. Nothing happened to this family until 1943 because they needed them – they needed him. And he didn't wear the Jewish star. His sons were in our school and were our friends and had to wear the Jewish star. It was the first time that I thought about the nonsense of the whole matter.

Burying the Dead

Paul Clüsserath was born in Bonn in 1931. He avoided military service at the end of the war by travelling to Thuringia to live with his aunt in the country. At the beginning of 1945 at the age of 13, he witnessed the death march of prisoners through his aunt's village near Jena from Buchenwald concentration camp.

I fled from Bonn to Thuringia and lived with my aunt on her farm and helped out. My uncle had been drafted, and my aunt was alone with a few cows on the farm. I experienced something horrible there that I'll never forget. The concentration camp Buchenwald was 40 kilometres away from the farm. Prisoners were forced to march back into the central part of Germany. There was a main road that went past the farm, and sixteen people had to be buried. That was my worst war experience.

Which people were they?

Jews, refugees, and foreigners. And we – young people – there weren't any men left in the village – buried them 20 metres away from the road in a deep hole. When the Americans arrived, these bodies had to be dug up again and buried in the cemetery. I hid in the woods for a week with a friend of mine – with whom I had sworn to be a blood brother – so that we wouldn't have to dig up the dead. That was the worst experience I had during the war along with the aerial bombings and being confronted with death.

How did these people die?

They were shot because they weren't able to march any further. They were too weak during the march and were executed on the side of the road. It was a long trail that was accompanied by SS soldiers and the march was on foot. The prisoners who weren't able to continue were shot. I heard that it was even worse in the neighbouring village.

German Camps

Marie-Augusta Heibel worked as a nurse at a military hospital in Poland in 1940. During this period, she heard about how Jews were marched off by SS guards and murdered.

We thought that we would be sent south, but no way, we were sent to the east. And we arrived in Poland. We were there for a good year – and when the war started with Russia, we experienced it first-hand. Right across the street was a squadron of German Stukas.[14] They made such a horrible noise when they whizzed over the roof of our barracks that we thought they would tear the roof off. And the next Russian city wasn't far away – actually it was still Poland – but Hitler and Stalin had divided up Poland back then. The Russians received the eastern half and we received the western half.

When I was in my laboratory late at night, I would hear shots. Since I come from an old hunting family, I can tell the difference between shots – whether those are shots from a machine gun, or a rifle, or whatever. In any case, after I had heard shooting every night – sometimes machine guns – sometimes single shots – I once asked the non-commissioned officer who was responsible for the barracks: "What's going on at night? Who's shooting out there?" At first, he was somewhat at a loss for words and said: "I really don't know, either. I've also heard it." I thought to myself: "This is really unpleasant. Someone ought to know what's going on. It's not here on the hospital grounds, but it's somewhere – you can hear it." And then finally I asked one of the doctors whom I had known from earlier – we had met just by chance there. "You hear it, too. What's going on here?" He said: "Jews are being shot."

Jews were being shot?

Jews were being shot. In fact, we were later in a small village – Augustów – which was 10 kilometres away from our military hospital – back then it was in Russian territory – but as I said only 10 kilometres away. There was a road with thick woods to the right and left – really thick woods – and you couldn't see through them. And there was a huge field – I'm not sure why I was able to go along – in any case, a girlfriend and I went along – it was a Polish hunting club – wonderfully situated in the woods. There were two large buildings: one was being converted into a sanatorium for wounded German officers, and the other was for the troops. A group of people in ragged clothes came towards us. Walking ahead of them was an SS man – wearing a field-grey uniform with the runic characters[15] – with the SS insignia here on the sleeve. That's what the Russians used to tell us later. They could always tell the exact difference between the SS and the regular army. They always said: "Bird here – good – which meant the regular army – bird here – bad." The SS men had an eagle on their sleeves besides the runic characters – while the regular army people had the eagle on their chest. That's the distinction that they made.

Oh, yes – there was this group of men – and curious as I always was – I asked someone: "Who are those people?" They had to suddenly start singing the "Horst Wessel Song".[16] You could see that they were Jews – although all Jews certainly do not look alike the way you imagined – with a crooked nose – and the way the Nazis portrayed them – so ugly that it almost hurt. They did that intentionally. But you were able to recognise these people. And in the village, there were a lot of Jewish families that lived there – and the SS only left the old men and women and children there. All the others were gathered together and had to work. I asked one of the SS men: "What are you doing with them? Why do they have to sing the 'Horst Wesel Song'?" He responded somewhat cocky: "We taught them that." And I said: "That's ridiculous. I thought that they were here to work and not to sing." He said: "Yes, they have to do that, too." In any case, he made it clear that they would be kept alive until the work was finished and then they would be shot. That's what he said to me.

Annelies Spiller was born in Katowice, Poland in 1923 as part of a German minority. During the war she worked for the Wehrmacht as an interpreter in German prisoner-of-war camp Stalag VIII-B for English soldiers in Silesia.

In 1942 I finished my Reich Labour Service and immediately went to Leipzig to a language school to study English for interpreting.

And when I returned home, my brother was there on his last leave, and I had to find a job. Besides, I was engaged. They wouldn't have allowed me not to work. I was engaged to an officer on night flights who shot at the English. We wanted to get married, but until then I had to stay busy. They wanted us to do something – you know – to contribute to the war effort. And we had an acquaintance who was at the Eighth Army Command in administration, the army headquarters in Breslau. And after I took my examination, he offered me a job in a prisoner-of-war camp for English soldiers in 1C [the main camp]. I started off the work by examining letters. We had to read through letters and cross things out. And if we were too lazy then we just put a stamp on the letters and approved them. We had to check incoming and outgoing letters. With the outgoing letters we had to be careful that there weren't more letters going out than coming in. Their wives wrote to them. For the first time, I saw that if they wanted to send kisses, they made little XXXs.

And soon I went to the department for account auditing. It was very interesting because there were a lot of different things to do. And then I worked in 1C [the main camp] in the reception room. The English had their own administration, and naturally their camp commander had contact [with the Germans]. They had a camp that was made up of simple soldiers and NCOs [non-commissioned officers]. And the NCOs had one person who took care of them: Sergeant Major Reed. And he had contact with the Germans. He told them what the NCOs didn't like – it was their right. And then he came to our German camp commander, to Captain Gylek, or to our 1C [main camp] – and I had to go along because I had to interpret so that they had a witness and so that they were certain that everything was interpreted correctly. We also had a military hospital with English doctors, and, as I said, Sergeant Major Reed was there. And then we had the protecting power that was visiting. The English had Switzerland as the protecting power. The Swiss had to come once or twice a year according to instructions by the Red Cross. And we had to leave them alone with the prisoners. They came there – this is important when I tell you about Auschwitz later. And then they came, and the prisoners could have everything they wanted. The only thing that we took away was clothing when they tried to escape. Do you know what I mean? When we caught them, we took away their clothing. And then we asked: "Why did you try to escape?" And they said: "Because I thought it my duty to do so." That was their excuse and nothing happened to them, unless they damaged something. You understand? They weren't allowed to damage anything while they were escaping – attack tanks or anything like that. That wasn't allowed. We had a court case once – that was horrible – and then that was quashed.

We had two English soldiers who threw stones into the machines at the Hermann Göring Plant next to the infamous Auschwitz camp – and, of course, that was sabotage. And then it started. They were imprisoned, and a long report was sent to our headquarters in Breslau to the Eighth Army Command. And from there the protective power was informed and came immediately because they knew what it meant. It was sabotage. And the Germans had them. The question was whether they would be executed or not. They were not sentenced to death. And next door – and this is something that you have to know because it is interesting for the difference between English and Russian prisoners – next door we had a prisoner-of-war camp for Russian soldiers. Our English prisoners were under the control of the German armed forces. The Russians were under the control of the SA. You can imagine what that meant. Of course, that was horrible. One time they caught a group of Russians – I believe that there were four or five of them – and they were sentenced to death by the SA. And they built gallows in our camp as a deterrent. We civilians were supposed to stay away on that Saturday, but the German soldiers who worked there were supposed to come. The Russians fled during the night. And I believe – they never found it out – but I believe that the English doctors helped them to get out – to flee. I'll never forget how they stood out there on that Saturday and hammered the gallows together and stood them up. That was horrible. The Russians were not part of the Geneva Convention. You know? And today they still aren't in the Geneva Convention and that's why the SA was able to take charge. And they did. The Russians were condemned to death, received bad food, and so on. The Russians heated the ovens in our barracks, and we placed bread under the coals for them. And they had to watch out when they went outside which guards were there so that they weren't searched. And then they kept the bread. That was a fierce matter, but, as I said, the Russians weren't in the Geneva Convention and couldn't do anything.

What did it look like inside the camp? Can you describe it?

I was never in the camp. We had our barracks. I saw a film about how they tried to dig their way out. But not in our camp. I think that it was in the air force camp that they tried to get out. In our camp, the English always complained. It was their good right. They complained about everything that they didn't like. They sent Reed to us to see whether matters needed to be negotiated or not. But they were not treated badly. They were prisoners and went on work detail. According to the Geneva Convention, normal soldiers had to work, the NCOs could work, and officers were not allowed to work. And all the NCOs who were captured in Dunkirk in the beginning of the war worked because they thought that life in the camps was ridiculous. As soon as the NCOs noticed that the war was going downhill for us, they stopped working. And we had to accept it because it was part of the Geneva Convention. Only the simple privates up to whatever rank worked.

And then we had a large group on work detail next to Auschwitz. There was the Bayer Plant and the Hermann Göring Plant in Auschwitz, and right next to it somewhere was Birkenau. You understand? And our English prisoners – and this is something that I've always wondered about – worked together with Jews in these plants. The English didn't mention ONE word about what had taken place in Birkenau – because they didn't know. Do you understand? And they also didn't say anything to the protecting power because the Swiss certainly would have said something to the NCOs or our C11C [subcamp] if the English had opened their mouths. They never said anything – never. Our first camp was in Lamsdorf, and then the camp was divided and we went down to Teschen. And Teschen is about 15 to 20 kilometres away from Auschwitz – no further than that. And the English never said one word about this, and after the war this was really on my mind. If they had known, then somewhere or somehow something would have been revealed. Surely. But not one word was said. The idiots came out when the airplanes flew overhead to bomb the plants. The stupid English came out with white towels and waved – I can understand that – but they were attacked. The bombs came down and they had a number of casualties. They should have stayed in their barracks.

Franz Birker was born in Solingen in 1927. He recalls the six weeks that he spent at the officers training school in Bergen-Belsen in 1945.

Three or four of us were sent to officers training school – and that was in Bergen-Belsen. The training area in Bergen-Belsen is approximately 25 kilometres wide and 3 kilometres long. It still exists today. Today, there are English troops that carry out their military exercises there. I was schooled in the last barrack. I marched past the concentration camp Bergen-Belsen every morning for six weeks without knowing what it was. I thought that it was a camp for French soldiers – who were also prisoners there. They had to repair the fence or do some kind of work. While I was marching past, I asked a fellow soldier from the region who was marching next me: "What is that actually? Is that a prisoner-of-war camp?" And he only said to me – and I'll never forget it: "Shut your mouth. If you talk about it, then you'll end up there." Of course, that aroused my curiosity.

I slowly discovered that it was the concentration camp Bergen-Belsen. I witnessed the transfer of concentration camp prisoners from the East because the Russians were advancing. Some of them were brought to the train station in Bergen-Belsen which was on the military training grounds. They had to walk the rest of the way – but this only took place at night. It was supposed to be as inconspicuous as possible. If there were air raids – the barracks didn't have any air-raid shelters – we had to go into the woods and saw this trail of misery passing by. They were guarded by the SS and dogs. Some of the concentration camp prisoners were being held up by one or two others so that they were able to walk along. That was the concentration camp Bergen-Belsen.

How were the prisoners treated?

I don't know. I only know that there was no systematic killing there. After the war, I heard from the Bergen-Belsen trials that the prisoners died of illness and hunger. At the very beginning before I started my six-week training, I was in one of the two gas chambers located on the premises near our barracks. It was a square room with spouts on the top and without windows. It was sealed off, and we were given gas masks to see whether they were airtight. If our eyes watered, we had to go outside. We waited a while, tried on another size, and did it again three or four times if necessary. At first, when we started at the officers training school, we were in the outer room of the concentration camp and our clothes were sterilized by means of steam, and we had to shower. We went to our barracks without knowing that the concentration camp prisoners also went through there. They also had to undress and shower, but we never spoke with any of those people.

Forced Labourers in the Eifel

Margrit Losenhausen was born in 1936 in Aachen. Her father was the forest ranger responsible for the Silberberg Lodge and the surrounding forest in the Eifel Mountains and was commissioned with the supervision of forced labourers from Ukraine and Russia for work in the forest. She recalls these prisoners of war from a childhood perspective.

The Russians came and became forest workers like the French before them, and my father had to supervise them. They came in early 1942 and were lodged in a double house called Silberberg II, which from then on served as a prisoner-of-war camp and a simplistic woodsman's dwelling. A little later Maria came to the house as a maid: At that time, she was a girl of 14 or 15 years of age in a padded grey jacket with dark brown, shiny braids. She trembled with fear that the forest ranger might defile her. Upon arrival, Maria descended from the open wagon into the freezing cold and cried. She was a forced labourer from Ukraine, came from Poltava, and learned German very quickly. "Marusya", as I called her, was a sweetheart whom we children approached with respectful love. She cooked delicious soup for us from hot buttermilk and cut raw potatoes into it which my father had grown at that time on the 10 acres of land.

Abdul, who was born a Tatar, and the only one of the group of Russians at the POW camp at Silberberg II who could read, drove me to school in Krekel, a small town in the Eifel, every day in a dog cart pulled by a double team of ponies. Abdul became my father's personal servant, so to speak; he read every wish from his eyes. My father organized a newspaper in Cyrillic, from which Abdul read aloud to his comrades every morning, sitting on the courtyard wall. They enjoyed smoking the "papirossi", which my father had also organized by the hundreds. In the meantime, our Russians had made themselves at home with us in the forest ranger's house, but at night they returned to Silberberg II.

Boris, whom everyone but us children were afraid of, operated the butter churn, which was filled every week with the sour cream from our four cows, while rhythmically pulling up his upper lip. Wassily carved toys for us children, for example a small wooden elephant that my smallest brother could ride on, or a "nodding dachshund" that still exists today in my home.

In the hot summer of 1944, our prisoners harvested vast quantities of raspberries while working and made raspberry brandy from them. This was done by means of a construction involving conservation pots sealed with bread mass and an ingenious tube system. In the summer of 1944, my father wisely had a log cabin built in a former quarry, which would ultimately ensure our survival. On Christmas 1944, we were surprised with carved toys from our dear prisoners. In return, wild game that my father had managed to put aside was served in the Silberberg II camp. I'll never forget the horrible New Year's Eve of 1944 in our Silberberg lodge: on the nearby road in the direction of Schmidtheim, the last vestiges of soldiers passed by. Child soldiers in oversized uniforms and steel helmets sang and happily marched through deep snow to their deaths. Soon afterwards, the execution squad came from Urft to gather together our Russians. Abdul, Wassily, and Boris were provided with food and inconspicuous clothing by my father, but it was all in vain. All these people were murdered, as my father later reported. We were able to hide Maria successfully. She was placed in my youngest brother's bed storage compartment in the log cabin for a short time, which was camouflaged with an oriental rug. After the war, she continued to serve us faithfully for many years. When she met a nice Polish man, she immigrated with him to America. Years later, she visited us again with her husband and child.

The Master Race

Dr Ingeborg von Plotho was born in Hamburg in 1919 and studied medicine at the University of Hamburg in 1942. She describes how the Nazis performed genetic research in order to create a master race. After the war, Dr Plotho worked as a neurologist and psychiatrist, and also provided psychoanalytic treatment to Jews who survived the atrocities of the Holocaust.

The Nazis managed the affairs of the universities. We knew exactly which professors were Nazis and which weren't. The director of the clinic, who was not a Nazi, had a key chain in his hand, and whenever he greeted us, he said "Heil Hitler!" and shook his keys. Nothing more than that. We had to greet one another with "Heil Hitler!"

Did the Nazis have an influence on the direction of medical research?

Oh, of course, they did. My supervisor in Hamburg was Professor Weiss, director of the Second Medical Clinic, and his wife's maiden name was von Verschuer. And Professor von Verschuer [my supervisor's father-in-law] was a very famous genetic researcher.[17] And he was controlled by the Nazis. I'm not sure to what extent he himself was a Nazi because he lived in Frankfurt or someplace else. I never met him, and I was never interested in his books because I basically found genetic research terribly boring. I was only interested in whether cancer or schizophrenia were hereditary. These were the things that interested me – so that we could help people and regulate the therapy. But this Professor von Verschuer was greatly supported by the Nazis so that they could determine which illnesses were hereditary, and then most of these people were supposed to be eradicated. Euthanasia for the mentally deficient, the feeble-minded, people with clubfoot – Goebbels himself had a clubfoot which came from a childhood paralysis – that is certainly a hereditary disease although I wasn't interested in that – and they exterminated the schizophrenics in a way that was horrible. [weeps] They killed them – feeble-minded children. Of course, they were a burden on the economy – there was very little to eat and so on and so on – and they killed them so that they wouldn't take away the food from the healthy.

This took place at the universities themselves?

Not at the universities – there were state institutions. There used to be a large state institution – it's still there – you'll see some beautiful old buildings – you really have to take a look at them – they're really beautiful. There were certain state clinics in Germany which were famous for killing people and sending letters to family members stating that a child had died from an appendix infection, and the ashes were sometimes sent home to the families in a vase. They wanted to eliminate useless or defective genetic material. They wanted to create a master race which knew everything and did everything wonderfully – and this was the Nordic race. The Nordic race allegedly had this wonderfully long skull. A half-Jewish girlfriend of mine, Resi Wolf, lived with her three sisters and her mother in Hamburg. Her Jewish father had already died, thank God. He didn't have to go through any more suffering. At first, they lived in Mecklenburg-Western Pomerania – and the teacher in the village there was a stupid Nazi – he drew on the children's heads to show what a real Aryan person looked like – with a long beautiful skull – and he took Resi's three sisters, who were amazingly attractive, and said: "That's the typical Aryan skull." And those were half-Jews. They didn't say anything, but anyone with a bit of knowledge knew that Jews often had the names Wolf and Wolfson, and so on. But this was not necessarily an indication that someone had to be Jewish. The Jews were not killed by the universities, or through research, but rather they were gathered together, transported, and murdered in Auschwitz or somewhere else. We know enough other stories describing how they did this. It was really very malicious. In Hamburg there were a lot of cultivated and relatively wealthy Jews who were able to emigrate on time. But in other cities, in Berlin and in central Germany, there were a lot of Eastern European Jews who didn't have enough money and didn't have the connections to

America and couldn't flee so quickly. And many people didn't want to. They wanted to stay in Germany. It was their home.

After the war I wrote psychological evaluations for many Jews, or, at least for some Jews. My supervisor strongly favoured compensating the Jews and determining the extent of the permanent psychological damage inflicted on them from the inhumane treatment in concentration camps – if they had managed to come out alive. But there were also professors, ones that I knew and respected, who claimed that when a person develops a depressive reaction or a depressive neurosis in his life, it is due to a predisposition and doesn't have anything to do with external circumstances – which is nonsense. If someone survives a concentration camp, then they suffer psychological damage such as depression and severe neurotic disorders. I always tried to arrange for these patients to get continued psychiatric treatment from their analysts in New York. This was paid by the German Restitution Office so that they would be able to live better with this therapeutic help. And this happened if we approved it in the evaluation. My supervisor, Professor Weitbrecht, was very much in favour of compensating patients who suffered from severe neurotic disorders. Either they received financial compensation or they received money needed for the psychiatrist or psychoanalyst. It was very difficult for many of them to trust us – to trust German doctors. But I think someone quickly notices whether a person is a fascist or anti-Nazi. And the Jews have an especially fine feeling for this. They have a sense for this – they know who is for them and likes Jews and values Jews. They know who is against the merciless slaughter that took place.

The Beginning of the War (September 1939)

Margaretha Harms was born in East Friesland in 1932. She remembers hearing the news of the war as a seven-year-old child.

I remember how the news of the war was announced. We were at my grandparents' farm. And there was a radio and then shouts: "War has broken out! War has broken out! And now we're going to win." The children danced around. We didn't know what it meant. I can remember that. And then it all started. My father was still young, but he was a miller. And millers were needed for baking bread and so on. He wasn't drafted until 1943 because he was a miller. He had a farm near us. And I lived in Extum near Aurich. He had to go to the mill and run the farm. I remember that. But afterwards he was drafted. We had four children in our family. And my brother was four years older. He left home and worked as an anti-aircraft helper.

And we had a bit of school. It was very difficult because we had to walk to the village. The worst thing was that we always had air-raid alarms and had to leave the school building. We were distributed among the farms when we left school. The school building was somewhat larger. And then there was a signal that all was clear, and we went back into the school building. Sometimes we had to work in the fields. That was from winter to summer, and we learned a little bit there. When we went to school there were low-flying fighter planes. We were a very large group of children who had to go to the cattle ground – that's what they used to call it. It was a small area there. And the low-flying planes often shot at us so that we went into ditches and dressed in light colours in the summer. I loaded my sister and myself down with wooden sticks. And then a milk truck came by that picked up the milk from the farmers. We were close to the carriage because we enjoyed hopping on the back of it. And the horses in front of the carriage were shot dead. I saw a horse bleed to death. That was horrible. That was terrible for a child to see.

Margrit Okrajek was born in Cottbus in 1924. She remembers the beginning of the war and the effect it had on her family and friends.

The abrupt change came in 1939. At that moment everything was over. My childhood was gone – the security, the whole family. I still haven't come to terms with it today. A sudden break came in our private lives. All the boys disappeared from their families because of the war. The harmony – the coming together – the patriarchal society shaped by farm life fell apart. It went well until this time. We even welcomed the campaign in France because Versailles played a significant role in the conversations with our parents. That was the revenge. And it was approved of and accepted. I had lots of cousins who were all immediately called up for military service. These were good boys who thought that Germany was in danger. They were dear boys, some of whom died in the war. My father wasn't drafted because he was too old. Our entire lives were suddenly turned upside down from one day to the next. At school, the boys in the parallel class were all sent to war. I grew up without boys or anything at all. In 1941, the catastrophe began. I was a 17-year-old girl and already knew that it was the end. I said to my mother: "We won't be able to withstand it. This is the end." And from 1940 onwards, all hell broke loose. We moved to Berlin and more or less spent all of our time in air-raid shelters. The American bombings have remained a trauma for me until today.

Helene Szeporniak was born in Katowice in Upper Silesia in 1930 as part of a German minority. She recalls the beginning of the war as a young girl at her school.

I was in a Polish school in the first and second grades, and it became a German school in the third grade when Hitler came to power. No matter whether you wanted to or not – all the children in Upper Silesia had to go to German schools. There weren't Polish schools anymore when the Germans arrived. These were the same schools, but with German teachers. [For example,] there was Mr Ehrlich from Hamburg. School was strict back then, and teachers were allowed to hit pupils. I was hit once, but that's the past now. The subjects were new: We had to learn how to read and write in German. We also used the Latin alphabet in Polish and so it wasn't that difficult. There were only a few letters that were different.

CHAPTER II

ALLIED BOMBINGS

Berlin

Wolfgang Koppe was born in Berlin in 1936. He remembers the bombing of the city from a child's perspective.

As a child, it was exciting for me to go into the air-raid shelter and see all the people together from our building. At that time, we lived in a three-story building of flats with about twenty families [which meant] forty people. And together with the people from the other building, there were fifty to eighty of us in the basement. [There was] a heavy iron door that closed behind us. We heard the bombs crashing down – sometimes we didn't hear them – because they were far away. And when we were allowed to leave the basement, we looked forward to the next day because we were able to collect bomb fragments. I remember having a large cigar box in which I collected these fragments, and I eagerly swapped them with my schoolmates. The largest and most strangely shaped fragments were worth the most.

Were you afraid?

No, at that time, I wasn't afraid at all. Even when the whole situation became more intense in 1942 and there were more air raids and the bombs fell right near us. My father extinguished a fire in a neighbour's house and was overcome by flames. And after spending some time in a hospital, he returned home very ill. But this didn't make me afraid. On the contrary, I was still somewhat enthusiastic about what I had heard from the older boys in our building who were already in the Hitler Youth. It was also my fondest wish to join the Hitler Youth. In 1946 I would have been old enough because you had to be 10 years old, but I never experienced it. The situation became more dramatic in the middle of 1942 or at the beginning of 1943 – I don't know anymore – the air raids were so frequent that the political leadership told us that mothers and children had to be evacuated from Berlin.

Berlin-Lichterfelde

Ursula Kamutzki was born in Berlin-Lichterfelde in 1924. She recalls the destruction of her family home through Allied bombings in 1943 and flight from Berlin after the death of her brother on the Eastern Front.

We had a large garden, and my father had a tennis court built. My parents really enjoyed playing tennis. And our neighbour was an SS officer. One day he came to us and said that if we gave up the tennis court, they would build an air-raid shelter there, and we would be able to use it. A group of Dutch prisoners came – very nice young men – and built the bunker for us. We were assigned a part of this bunker where we could put our things. And when there were air raids, we went inside with our neighbours – as many as could fit inside. It might have saved our lives, but our previous quality of life was over. There was no gas, no water, no lights – and there was something like iron curtains.

My father was from Sorau. My grandfather was the director of an administrative office there and had a house for my father. A pastor was living there at that time, and he took us in. And we stayed there until we fled from the Russians. We heard the gunfire. Nobody thought that the Russians would be able to penetrate so far into Germany. Even when we heard gunfire, we thought to ourselves: “That’s not possible. It can’t be them.” It was impossible to understand. And I had both of my parents with me. My mother had Parkinson’s and was seriously ill. And, at that time, my father was also ill. And whatever I was able to carry was everything that we had for the next stop. And we went to relatives in Halle an der Saale, which is also in eastern Germany. We had a room on the fourth floor and had to bring the suitcases up there. And my mother had to go up and down. It was horrible. And then finally, we got a room in Naumburg. On the day after we left, Halle was bombed, and we had just got out in time. We had lived in Halle a few months, and then we moved to Naumburg. We didn’t have anything anymore.

The locals had their contacts with the local businessmen, but we were strangers. My mother picked out a bit of jewellery and bartered with the Russians. It was normally the rations officer in Naumburg. And we hung up sausages behind father's bed on a rod. We hung them there so that the neighbours wouldn't be able to see anything because that would have caused trouble. Well, that was the time in Naumburg.

My father couldn't return to Berlin because his law office at Tiergarten and our house had burned to the ground. He applied and received a job as a district judge in Querfurt. We moved there in January 1946. It was the first time that we had a flat for ourselves. There was nothing in it, but we got the old furniture from the people who had left the farmhouse and moved west. My father started work in January 1946 and in May he lay down and was dead within four days. He had peritonitis. He had stomach pains during the whole time that we were fleeing, but we couldn't do anything about it. Well, my mother and I were left on our own. I still ask myself today how we managed. My mother was paralysed and could only move from the armchair to bed and back again. I had to help her move her head on the pillow. That's how incapable she was of helping herself. And, as her assistant, I at least received medical insurance.

Bochum

Marie-Luise Uphoff was born in Eickhoff near Minden in North Rhine-Westphalia in 1923. She recalls the bombing of the Bergmannsheil Hospital in Bochum where she worked as a nurse in 1944.

Bochum was bombed on three Saturdays. 4 November was the second attack. A week earlier – seven days before 4 November – was the first attack. We were in the middle of the city and worked like crazy because all the injured people were brought to us. On the next Saturday – on 4 November – we ourselves were bombed. Flattened. There wasn't anything left. One of our nurses and thirteen children were killed. The third attack came one week later when we were already in Bochum-Langendreer. They flattened Bochum on three consecutive Saturdays. It was really flattened.

Can you remember all three attacks?

I can remember the second attack the best. During the first one we didn't know what hit us because one patient after the other was brought to us. And that was during a period when I was working in the operating room. We worked throughout the entire night. There were all kinds of injuries – amputations – everything. It's not possible to describe all of it.

What happened on 4 November?

That was at 7:00 pm. It was always at 7:00 pm. The sirens went off and the bombs were dropped and people made sure that they hid in the tunnels. I was getting ready to go home – work was over in the operating room – and we didn't have any more work. Bandages had to be rolled up and other things [taken care of]. I wanted to go to the nurses' house when the attack started. We all knelt down in a circle with our faces to the ground and promised one another that we wouldn't argue anymore. We were all young girls. [laughs] Afterwards, it was over. It was quiet. But it was burning all over. My aunt tried to come to me from Langendreer – because she lived in Langendreer. She wasn't a real aunt, but she came to my parents during the summer holidays in 1917 and all of us liked her a great deal. She tried to get to the Bergmannsheil Hospital in Bochum for three days. And then she found me.

It's impossible to describe how the attacks were when you were sitting in a basement and heard the bombings. In the basement there were only the bare necessities with benches on the sides and otherwise nothing. In the tunnels it looked a bit different: the senior staff brought the beds down every evening and placed them next to one another. They came every evening and brought the patients down there. In the morning they came again and brought them upstairs again. This is because the patients couldn't walk. They only took care of the bed-ridden patients, and the others had to see how they got along. The sad thing was that people working on the excavation tried to find survivors, and one father was there who held the head of his child in his hands and the body was still buried. And I'm still embarrassed today for what I did. We had to bring the dead bodies to the morgue. And I left because I couldn't … because I … I was a coward. The others continued working, but I didn't.

Bonn

Helga Steeg was born in Bonn in 1927. She recalls the bombing of Bonn in October and December 1944.

It was horrible during the war because of the continuous bombings. At night you always had to stay in the basement. On 18 October 1944, the entire Old Town was destroyed – the entire Old Town was destroyed and it burned for days. The town hall burned, the market burned, and all the houses on Wenzelgasse and Brüdergasse burned. It was one big inferno. And there were several other major air raids such as on 21 December 1944. On Berlin Street, which is today called Prinz-Albert Street and where the Elisabeth Hospital is located, we had a large flat in a beautiful old house that was destroyed. During this time, in December 1944, the schools were closed. And I was in high school and was supposed to graduate in 1945. The schools were not only closed, but many of my schoolmates were sent to the Siegfried Line in the west in order to help out.[1] And I had a … how shall I phrase it … a very energetic mother, and she made sure that I went to work – my sister was too small and didn't have to work.

And I worked as a conductor on the buses in Bonn. This wasn't that much fun because sometimes there were air raids and bombs were dropped. But, in spite of that, I learned how to deal with people in a friendly way. I did this in the summer of 1944. In the summer of 1943, I worked as a mail carrier in Cologne instead of spending my holidays at a resort place. We were brought there by bus in the morning and returned in the afternoon and had to deliver the mail in the extremely bombed-out city of Cologne. I learned several different professions in my life. In 1945 I should have graduated from high school, but it was impossible because everything had been destroyed. The university was destroyed and burned out – completely burned out. And the law faculty had been moved to the Education Centre in Bad Godesberg. My high school class – as well as soldiers who came back from the war without a high school diploma because they had been drafted – had to enrol in a special course. We were able to get our General Equivalency [GCSC] between October 1945 and May 1946, but it was freezing in the schools. We had to bring along coal briquettes and sat there in completely bombed-out schools. There was also a shortage of schools. We had to alternate between mornings and evenings. Those were horrible times.

Did the city continue to function although everything had been bombed? Was public transportation still working?

Yes. Yes. Yes. More or less. The buses used wood for fuel. I'm not sure how the process worked, but in the back of the buses there were ovens that burned wood which allowed the buses to drive. And the trams also worked as if everything hadn't just been destroyed. As I mentioned before, there was a major air raid in October 1944 and the buses and trams didn't work anymore in the Old Town. Everything had been levelled to the ground – everything had been levelled to the ground. Relatively little happened to the present-day western and southern part of the city – a little bit, but not very much – but the old city centre was destroyed. The university was destroyed. The various university institutes in Poppelsdorf were burned out. All of it was a wasteland.

Where did people go from the Old Town?

A lot of them died, of course. A lot of them were killed from the fires and the bombs. Beginning in 1943, the Nazis started evacuating children to the middle of Germany in the east. Many of them fled to or the middle of Germany that later became the GDR. Our young lives had been destroyed. In spite of that, I was enrolled in a dance course. And we had a dance course in the destroyed Old Town, and I had my first motor scooter. These things happened too, you know. The closer the war came to an end, the less we met with friends and went dancing. Now and then, there were bombings. And then everything was cleaned up again because people tried to continue with their lives by mid-1944. The boys were anti-aircraft helpers. We were bus conductors or mail carriers. Two of my schoolmates were anti-aircraft helpers in Berlin.

Otto Graf Lambsdorff,[2] who was a friend of mine at university, was also an anti-aircraft helper and lost his leg on 20 April 1945 – I don't know where that was – maybe in Leipzig – in any case, he only had one leg. But he was pro-American and became an important man, you know. Things like this happened.

I can't say that you forget those things, but when you talk about it then you remember those things. Our young days were not a time of adolescence. Of course, after the war was over, we were able to celebrate although there was nothing to eat. At the university of Bonn, there were students who came from the Saarland and brought along wine with them. And our mothers baked cakes. We celebrated because there was a feeling of liberation after the horrible things in the war. And we enjoyed life. But all of us finished our studies very quickly. Not in twenty semesters. We were done in six semesters.

Near the end of the war, Aachen changed hands several times. The Americans came and took it, and then the Nazis won it back again. And for this reason, there were a lot of refugees who moved in the direction of the east. I remember this well. The refugees moved to Friedrichstraße and Friedensplatz, which was called Adolf Hitler Platz at that time and was the favourite street for farmers or other people who came and fled from these occupied areas. And then the bombings during the night, and the bombs that fell during the day, were horrible. In the last few weeks before the Americans came, we didn't even bother getting undressed to go to bed. Everyone had a bag with the most important things that they brought along to the basement. Today it's impossible to imagine this. And that's why there were no celebrations at that time. And all our boys were away at war – either as anti-aircraft helpers or in the real war.

When did the American soldiers finally arrive?

They arrived in Bad Godesberg on 8 March 1945. Our family home had been bombed out, and we then lived with relatives on Dengler Street in Bad Godesberg. In the house across the street there were friends of our relatives – my mother's brother and my aunt. And we went to the air-raid shelter. My relatives lived in a new house with a modern basement, and across the street they had an old basement. Bombs continued to fall on Bonn, Wesseling, and Cologne. It was horrible.

They were all afraid. They went into the basements because they were afraid that it would happen here, too. And one morning, the telephone rang and it was someone with an excited voice. And this friend of our relatives was the mayor of Bad Godesberg – not a Nazi mayor, but rather an administrative mayor. And he said to my mother that the Americans had told him that if Godesberg didn't surrender in – I don't know – one or two hours then it would be fired upon. My mother spoke English very well and interpreted for the mayor who of course didn't want to reveal his whereabouts. But they found this out. And then she went with the mayor to the top of Bad Godesberg where the Americans were staying. It was a dramatic situation. The military command was in Hotel Dreesen. And that must have been very dramatic. The military didn't want to surrender the city – but we didn't know exactly what happened because we weren't along. And the Swiss General Consul who lived on Roland Street was there as well. In any case, the city of Bad Godesberg surrendered peacefully and was not fired upon. And then the Americans came – I remember this precisely – in their military uniforms. We lived on Dengler Street with our relatives, and they came through in lines. Several people hung flags outside and were happy that it was all over. However, there were still German soldiers on the other side of the Rhine who fought for a long time. And then the famous Bridge of Remagen was fired upon.

Hilde Dahm was born in Bonn in 1913. She recalls the bombings of Bonn in 1944.

I lived on Heer Street on the corner of Dorotheen Street. There was a woman who had completely lost her mind. She must have lost relatives, and it was burning everywhere. She didn't stop screaming. She screamed and screamed and kept on running. She was totally insane. She probably lost family members. She ran all the way down Heer Street. And then I didn't see her anymore. Horrible. Horrible.

There were ten children in our family. Three died in the war. And one sister was killed during the bombings on Bahnhof Street. There was an electrical appliance store – oh, what was the name of that again? All the people in that building died. They had a security service which claimed that nothing would happen to anyone because they had the best equipment. Three children and all the employees were there. The only one who wasn't there was the trainee. My sister told her: "You go to the air-raid shelter." Another person said: "How can you decide for her?" And my sister answered: "She's my trainee, and she's going to the air-raid shelter." My sister and all the others were killed. The bombs fell and that was the end.

My mother was more afraid for me because I never went into the basement. But nothing happened to me. It took me two hours to go from Münster Square to Breite Street. Can you imagine that? It was burning everywhere, and you couldn't get through. It was burning everywhere. And the people were screaming – it was horrible – I can still hear it today. Horrible! Bonn was in rubble. I was amazed that the Münster Church was still standing. Otherwise, everything on Münster Square had been destroyed. The post office on Münster Square was almost completely destroyed. And Münster School – that's where I went to school – it was awful. What a mess the Nazis made! And nothing happened to them. They snuck away early. The horde of pigs.

Elisabeth Schneider was born in East Prussia in 1922. She recalls attacks from Allied bombers while living with her two children in Bonn.

The low-flying planes were the worst thing in the war. I have two girls. One of them was a few months old, and the other was over a year. They had whooping cough. A doctor arranged for them to go to Nonnenwerth – an island [in the Rhine] – to the hospital in the convent. She arranged for the children to go there. I had to go to Nonnenwerth every day – on foot. Cars stopped at the Reuter Bridge. Someone was standing there and stopped the cars and asked them where they were going. If they were going in a certain direction, then they had to take you along. And this went on for weeks. I went there every second day.

One day, the nurse told me: "Mrs Schneider, you have to take your children home with you. The entire hospital is being evacuated." I was on foot so I picked up the children one at a time. Cars stopped along the way. On the next day, I picked up the other child. I had to walk a long distance or someone took me along. The airplanes came, and I had to go into the bushes and lie down. They were flying low. And then the children were at home, and the air-raid alarms started ... That was the worst time for me – with the children.

Cologne

Hannelore Füssenich was born in Cologne in 1923. She recalls the bombing of the city by English war planes in 1942 and 1943.

I was in Cologne for the entire war. The bombings were terrible. I experienced the biggest attack on Cologne, but I don't remember when it was anymore. Everything was completely destroyed. I was invited to a birthday in Braunsfeld in Cologne and was on my way home in the evening. And then the bombings started. They came one after the other. First, there was always a siren. It sounded for a long time – it sounded for a long time – three times in a row. And then we knew that the planes were on their way. But then the siren sounded in very short intervals. This meant that the planes were already there. And I lay down in the bushes on the Aachener Weiher [city park] because everything in the downtown area of Cologne, the opera house, had been destroyed by bombs. That was such an inferno. That was the biggest air raid ever.

I personally experienced this air raid and many others as well. I can't even tell you how many times I lay on the ground with my hands covering my head. And in air-raid shelters. We always went to bed with our clothes on with all the necessities next to us and then went to the air-raid shelters. Everyone was excited in the shelters. At this time, there was hardly anything to buy, but there was tobacco. And I rolled cigarettes for the men and the women to smoke. And that's how I started smoking at the age of 16. People were nervous and afraid.

Did people speak in the air-raid shelters or was there absolute silence?

At the beginning it was quiet. I always went to the shelter with my mother. These shelters were organized according to streets. Of course, the windows all had to be blackened, and you weren't allowed to have any lights on. And there were so-called "local Nazi Party leaders". They were holier than the Pope. They were the worst ones. They were the worst ones. If there was a little bit of light, then it was enough to call the Gestapo. They were responsible for order so that everything was dark. There was often a signal that everything was clear. All of us went back upstairs to bed, and then the siren sounded again. And we all had to go back down again. And then there was another air raid.

Afterwards we moved from the downtown area to Cologne-Thielenbruch. That's on the outskirts of the city. I always rode on my bike from Cologne-Thielenbruch to Braunsfeld and there were always air raids on the way. One time, I experienced an air raid in Cologne-Mühlheim on the Mühlheim Bridge. I arrived just after an air raid, and there were arms and legs all over the place. The English dived down in their planes and fired at people. They fired directly at groups of people. That's the way it was.

Did this happen late in the war?

This was in the middle of the war in 1942 or 1943. By the way, my brother was drafted when he was 20 years old. I still have the letter from his commander. He was along during the invasion [of Russia], and they didn't find any of his remains. He disappeared without a trace. Would you be interested in the letter? He was part of the advanced guard of a tank unit and was trampled into the ground.

Yes, of course.

My father wanted to travel from Düsseldorf to Duisburg. He left his car parked in the garage and went by train. And a low-flying English plane came and fired on the train. A piece of shrapnel hit my father on the temple and killed him. And then there was the great evacuation, and my whole family was evacuated to Mühlhausen in Thuringia. I was employed by a lawyer who was working on damages from the war. And I was important for the war effort and wasn't allowed to leave. Whenever there were bombings, we had to compile lists of things that had been destroyed. And this list was presented to the War Damage Office in

Cologne in the Trade Fair Centre, and people received compensation for everything that had been destroyed. They always received an initial three thousand Reichsmarks.

How could they afford to compensate all those people?

I don't know, but they got this amount. Three thousand Reichsmarks. People lost much more. This was only initial compensation.

Dresden

Mechtild von Holtey was born in 1924 in Giesmannsdorf in the district of Bunzlau in Silesia. During the war she studied at the University of Leipzig. She recalls the bombing of Dresden.

The people of Dresden were convinced that they would be spared the bombings because Dresden was considered an international art city. And they were right. You can still see that today – I have pictures somewhere. You can see how much art there was when you look at the centre of the city and the Elbe. You can see how much art there was in terms of the buildings. They have rebuilt many things there like the opera house. Dresden was still basically my home, and in Leipzig and in other cities in the west I was a student. In Dresden I lived in our family flat that was close to the Großer Garten [city park] which was very beautiful and important. We lived on a street parallel to the Großer Garten. And, of course, that was our escape route when the bombers attacked the houses and the streets filled with people. Once you were in the city, it was very difficult to escape although the Elbe went right through the middle of the city, and the city centre was what they called the "Old Town". The new part of Dresden was on the other side of the Elbe, and that's where I went to school. I always had a long way to school. I began with French in Halle on the Saale, and the school in the new part of Dresden was the only one where you could begin with French. When I was in my third year of secondary school, my father was transferred to Dresden, and that's why we were there. But the confidence that people had was enormous – "nothing will happen to us" – although Leipzig was very often attacked. "They won't dare to attack Dresden with all the art treasures." It was naive.

Afterwards there were four major air raids at night. I think that it was in February 1944. There weren't many air raids – but these few air raids were enough to level Dresden – the inner city. Every house had to have its own air-raid shelter. Those were regulations. People couldn't just do what they wanted and say: "I don't care. That doesn't interest me." There were authorities in each city – I've forgotten what they were called – the people who were responsible for maintaining order in a city. We also had an air-raid shelter. But the question was how prepared were we to move with all our belongings and start again. And this is what happened to everyone who was living in the inner city of Dresden. There were very few buildings that were still standing. Well, at that point in time – on that evening when it began – it lasted for four consecutive nights – I was in Leipzig. The bombings were different there. I know that a friend of ours was supposed to get married, and the wedding had been planned. During the night, bombs were dropped on Leipzig. And all the guests who were invited – none of them paid with their lives – but they arrived in their bathrobes or whatever they could take along from their hotel rooms. Those were horrible times back then.

What I remember in particular – and it was the most unpleasant thing – was when the planes were gone, you came out from the basements – like in Leipzig when we had to take shelter in the buildings – and the first thing that you noticed was the smell of smoke. You couldn't go near the fires when the flames were high, but afterwards they died down and that was horrible. Everywhere there were remnants of fire. That was something unpleasant which you remembered. Much later when the war was over, I lived together with another family. But I didn't experience it the way that my mother and brother did because they didn't have anything anymore. They left the air-raid shelter and went to the Großer Garten because they knew that bombs wouldn't be dropped on the Großer Garten. You didn't know whether they [the bombers] were gone, whether they were still there, or whether they would come back. And that was from the first night on. I don't know when our flat was uninhabitable. Two years later I came to see our street. Our entire side of the street was gone. And on the other side of the street, there was a small cute villa that I could see from my window. That was still there. Otherwise, there wasn't much left. We had a house that was several stories high, and these houses extended down the street. And on the corner of the street there was a beautiful tennis court that was an ice rink in the winter. And the side street went directly to the Großer Garten. That's where they saved their lives and everything that they had with them. That's the horrible thing – that people didn't have anything left from their homes.

We had beautiful old furniture – but we weren't able to save it. One thing that we had in the basement – in the air-raid shelter – and it was a great attraction afterwards – was a large wooden barrel. Because while we were living in Halle, my father worked for a sugar refinery. And every Christmas we received a huge barrel [of sugar] – I think that it was half full – which was standing in our basement. And that's where we had our china. Not me, but rather my mother. It was valuable china. Each piece was individually wrapped and placed in this barrel in the basement. And after the war these items were sent individually to Weimar, where my grandfather still lived together with his housekeeper. Nothing happened to them although Weimar had also been bombed. In any case, the china was saved. And they also sent each plate individually to the west. And that is the good china that I still have today.

Emden

Hermann Harms was born in Neu-Ekels near Aurich (Lower Saxony) in 1930. He remembers the bombing of Emden at the age of 14.

I was doing a traineeship in Loga which is part of the city Leer. On 6 September 1944 – I remember the date exactly – there was a major air strike on Emden. We were in the Hitler Youth and had to help pick up rubble from the air raid on the following day and fill bomb craters and so on. There I experienced first-hand how the city of Emden had been destroyed. Emden was a strategic city because it was an important port on the North Sea. And I know – and it also surprised us – that the port facilities were not destroyed or bombed. Maybe we thought about these things at that time, or maybe we thought about them later. The English – or our enemies in the war – were interested in keeping our ports intact in order to be able to use them after the landing. I believe that a large part of Emden was destroyed – a very large part. The entire downtown area was gone – and surrounding areas as well. Emden had suffered horribly under this major strike. The railway facilities where we were working were also heavily affected. We lived approximately 20 kilometres away from Emden.

Emmerich

Karla Geinert was born in Emmerich on the Rhine in 1924. She returned home from Reich Labour Service and witnessed the complete destruction of the city by English bombers on 7 October 1944.

Emmerich was a small town with 40,000 inhabitants, but with a tremendous industrial potential. There were really famous large factories there. For example, Pelikan ink – no, back then it was Gimborn ink. It was world famous. The largest paper factory in Germany at that time was in Emmerich. Industry is always established on the water, and Emmerich is located on the Rhine. And it became a member of the Hanseatic League early on, which is very unusual for a small river town. I can't list all the companies, although I would like to because it is important for my life. There was a chocolate factory called Lohmann. As children we never had enough pocket money because we bought so much chocolate. [laughs] Then there was a cable factory. Then there was an ironworks factory, and they manufactured packaging for coal and briquettes. And, among other things, all the art nouveau facades, and the railings which were built for villas. These things came from this factory. Then we had something very important – I'm not going to list all the others – the famous Bols liqueur factory. On the Lower Rhine people drank beer, and that's the reason why they're stocky and stout – not like wine drinkers who are thin. And the Bols liqueur factory had a worldwide reputation. If you research these names, then you'll find out that they're correct. And what was extremely interesting was that at the entrance to the city, and at the end of the city, there were two companies which were financed with foreign capital. Unilever is still there today and Van der Laane. American and Dutch money was invested there and so on. And these two factories were damaged minimally during the air raids. The entire bombings took place between these two points. Ninety-three percent of the city was devastated. This aspect of the war is never mentioned.

I came back to Emmerich, but my mother had already moved to her relatives in the country. But, as I said, we always had people staying in our house. And I stayed in Emmerich because I hadn't seen my girlfriend from school for such a long time. She didn't have to serve in the Emergency War Service [Kriegshilfsdienst] because of family matters. It was autumn, and the weather was beautiful just like this year. And then suddenly one Saturday afternoon the sirens went off. There was an alarm the whole time. But if it was louder, for the highest danger, then the sound was different. The day was so beautiful. My relatives stored their porcelain on the farm in the country because it often broke. I took my bicycle and thought that I would bring them the porcelain and say hello to my mother. But first I rode my bike to my girlfriend's. I was in the basement with them during these eight days when there were air-raid alarms. And, on this day, I went to see them because the sun was so nice. And their village was six kilometres away from Emmerich. And then, from the road, I saw how the city was levelled. I also saw how the low-flying planes shot at moving objects – at people. The handlebars of my bicycle were so bright and reflected in the sun. [On either side of the road] there were ditches for the rainwater and groundwater that went into a drainage pipe. And I crawled inside it with my bicycle. The bicycle wouldn't fit. But I crawled into this drainage pipe. I was so clever, I have to say, that I pulled the reflecting handlebars into the drainage pipe. And the rest of the bicycle didn't reflect as much as the handlebars. I have to tell you that I watched how the whole city was levelled with high-explosive bombs and afterwards with phosphorous bombs. Our house withstood it, but the phosphorous bombs burned out the inside of the house. The walls remained standing. The people who were in the basements survived. But in the city quite a few people died. In particular, they got stuck in the melted asphalt. The only ones who had a chance were the ones who went quickly to the Rhine. There was air there. And, as I said at the beginning, the bombing raids took place between these two foreign capital factories. They remained standing almost totally intact.

Did you stay in the city after this day?

There wasn't anything left. I kept on going. I took my bicycle and turned around and kept on riding in the direction of Emmerich as far as the country road was still intact in order to see what had happened to my father. My mother was in the village, but my father was there and my middle sister was working in the paper factory during the holidays. I wanted to know what had become of her because I saw that it wasn't burning there. This factory on the Lower Rhine was built very solidly with burned clinker and so on. Many walls remained standing. They remained there. It was amazing that they didn't get buried in the rubble. They wet blankets and threw them over themselves and moved on in the direction of the Rhine as far as they could.

My father also survived, but without any eyebrows or hair on his head. And his clothes were singed and so on. And afterwards he complained – you can see how abnormally people behave sometimes. He wasn't really worried about our house. He only said that he went past the coat rack where his hunting rifles were hanging and wished that he had taken one of his beautiful rifles along. [laughs] These are simply spontaneous actions, but he also said this later. The neighbours told my mother that it was amazing that she survived so well. She had lost everything within half an hour's time that generations had saved for. You know that farmers have wars of succession [for property]. My mother's response to the bombings was, "So what? I still have my children." As simple as that. Right? In our circle of acquaintances, and among our relatives, and in the city, there were so many who had fallen in the war or were injured. Nobody ever said anything about it again. People accepted it because my mother was strong. It was her innermost wish [that everyone survived]. She always said: "Hopefully, they'll all come home safely again." And nobody from my immediate family died [in the war].

Frankfurt-Hanau

Erika Langenberg was born in Neisse in Upper Silesia in 1919 and spent her childhood in Frankfurt-Hanau. She recalls the devastating bombing of Hanau on 20 March 1945.

Hanau – 20 kilometres from Frankfurt – was first bombed in 1941. And then the night-time bombings started, and we wondered whether we would be able to sleep or not. We didn't have an air-raid shelter. During that time, I joined the Red Cross and was on duty at the military hospital and at the train station to take care of the wounded soldiers when they arrived. The train once arrived with wounded soldiers who had been travelling a long time. And I took care of a soldier who had leg injuries, and his shoe was open in the front. When we took off his bandage, maggots crawled out between his toes because there hadn't been the possibility to make up his bandage fresh again. And while I was on duty at the train station, there was a major air raid and the sirens went off. We three nurses brought 20 soldiers, who were just able to walk, into the basement of a brewery, which was about eight minutes away from the train station. In the sky, there were flares that floated down with small parachutes so that they could see where they were supposed to drop the bombs. And while we were on the way, the soldiers wanted to run away. They didn't want to go to some basement, but rather wanted to dig in outside like during battle. There was great chaos. We sat in this air-raid shelter and heard "clack, clack, clack, clack". Those were the fire bombs that were dropped, but did not penetrate. However, this noise haunted me later whenever I walked through a railway underpass and a train drove overhead.

And then there was the last major air raid – it was on 20 March 1945, shortly before the end of the war. My father had been drafted, and we didn't know where he was. Mother, another woman, and I were alone in the house. And my mother and I listened to the English radio broadcast with a blanket over us and so on. And they said that everyone in Hanau should make sure to leave the city. A major air raid was planned. We went to bed with our clothes on and had our suitcases next to us with all the important documents. And we thought: "Well, maybe we can sleep a little." And then suddenly, we heard a lot of bombs – a lot of airplanes. And we thought that retaliation was coming. And we quickly looked out the window shutters, and everything was red and the bombs were falling. We went downstairs into the basement. My mother, the woman, and I held each other and prayed. Everything was shaking. It was a sturdy old house. And then it was over. In the air-raid shelter, there were two iron staircases and an iron door that you had to open to get to the hatch. The hatch opened up entirely inward. In the front yard, there was an espalier fruit tree – you know fine fruit that was grown small. The fruit was lit up brightly and burned from the phosphorus. They had dropped phosphorous bombs. And then I helped my mother get out. She had to go along the side of the house because phosphorus was coming down from the flora. And then it was Mrs Müller's turn. And then I came out.

It was horrible. We went to the neighbour's house where nothing had happened. And our house was burning – it was ablaze. Soldiers came and then everything was quiet. A group of soldiers came to see if anyone had been injured. I was outside, and they asked whether anyone was in the basement. I said: "No." And I saw my mother standing in front of the old oak door of our house, trying to go back inside. It was impossible, you know? Everything was burning. I saw my bed upstairs with my teddy – it was an inferno. And as a Red Cross nurse, I had to go along downtown and recover the dead bodies. The bodies were burned so small [with her hands she shows 60 centimetres in length] from the phosphorus. It was dreadful. And we didn't have anything anymore. My aunt came from Rückingen near Langendiebach which is eight kilometres away – that was an airfield before – with a cart for me and my mother. Those were all the things that we had when we were evacuated. And 93 or 94 per cent of Hanau was destroyed. Frankfurt, too. It was awful.

Idar-Oberstein

Elsbeth Jansen was born in 1913 in Idar-Oberstein in Rhineland-Palatinate. In 1942, she returned to her parents' house with her two children to escape the bombings of the major cities along the Rhine. She recalls one incident that saved her children from death.

In 1942, I moved to my parents' house and lived there the whole time. We thought that it was safe there. But I always told my children that if there were a lot of bomber planes then I wanted them at home and not to go anywhere.

And afterwards we had an experience that I have to tell you about: My eldest daughter came home from school with her grandfather one day. My father taught my children because he had to keep working as a school teacher during the war. And then my eldest daughter came to me and said: "Can I go to my friend's house? Her mother said that we can play in their garden." And I didn't give her permission because there were so many bombers around. And that was fate – an act of providence – I have to say – I can't put into words. My daughter's friend and her mother were killed on that day because a bomber attacked the small village. The name of the village was Kirchdorf. Today it's a small town and not a farming community anymore. It now also has industry.

I believe that the Americans were on their way home and wanted to get rid of their bombs so they dropped cluster bombs onto the small village. There were eighteen deaths, and in one house a mother and her two children were killed. Isn't that unbelievable? What a fate! I had a premonition in which I had felt that was going to happen. Afterwards, we always went to the cemetery whenever we were in the town.

Kassel

Ilse Wolf was born in 1929 in Aschaffenburg. She remembers the bombing of Kassel in 1942 at the age of 13.

My parents' house was bombed in two daytime air raids, and we moved to the country. And from this village, I kept on going to school in Kassel. On 22 October 1942, there was a large air raid on Kassel in which the entire city was destroyed. My father had a small flat in the city, and we lived in the village. And on this evening, I had the task of sitting in my school as a "fire-guard" at the age of 14. I was supposed to do that with a girlfriend, and, at first, we found it all very exciting. But, in the meantime, there was this air raid. I told my mother that I had to go there because I had duty that day. That's the way we were. Then, for three hours, I ran through Kassel, which was burning and destroyed, in order to get to my father. I stood in front of my school, and the flames blazed from the building. And naturally I cried. When we were children, we would always say: "What would happen if a bomb fell on the school?" It was very bad, and we really experienced horrible things.

Weeks later they were still rescuing people from their basements. They came out with eyes like this. [She shows a frozen stare with eyes wide open.] Everywhere there was coal. And when you walked past the rubble and looked into the basement windows, you could see the blue flames burning the coal. And people were down there. And one time I had to get a mother out of there who we couldn't see anymore. Her child had died on her lap. And those were really horrible things for us at the age of 14.

Oh, yes. I remember that a week later there was a pile of bodies on the large square in Kassel, which was as high as a two-story house. Bodies were piled on one another. That was in 1943. Everything was destroyed. There was a group of us who were friends, and one of the girls was somewhat older. Her father was in France as a soldier and brought her back a wonderful violet-coloured leather bag. We were all very envious of her. And [I remember her] standing against the rubble of her house, and the bag was the only thing that remained. That was horrible for a 14-year-old girl.

All the schools were destroyed and were relocated somewhere in the country. And my school and my class were moved near Fulda, and then it got worse because the low-flying flights started. Of course, we were horribly afraid of them. For example, we had to go to the dentist in the neighbouring town and took the country road. The low-flying planes came along and riddled people with bullets. Those were fast English and American fighter bombers. Normally they accompanied groups of large bombers, and then they carried out low-flying flights and fired at trains and individuals. War takes place on both sides. It's a horrible thing. And I experienced it. We dived into the ditches along the road so that they wouldn't see us. It always took place between 11:00 am and midnight. We were really afraid. That's clear.

CHAPTER III

RETREAT FROM THE EAST

Evacuation of the Children

Franziska Haenert worked in the Kinderlandverschickung (Evacuation of the Children) in the annexed territory of Czechoslovakia. In August 1944, she was forced to flee with 4,000 school children across the Tatra Mountains through Poland on the way back to Germany.

The Kinderlandverschickung [KLV] was something very sensible – I say so today – and others would say it as well. There were constant air raids here in the west, and the schools were closed so that nothing would happen to the children. And school lessons weren't possible with children who had to go to air-raid shelters every night. The schools were closed and entire schools were moved to resort areas – in Bavaria – in the large hotels in resort areas. Entire schools with teachers and children were moved there. They turned the hotel rooms into dormitories – as I said, this was in resorts all over Bavaria and in other places – and sometimes they were military hospitals or KLV camps. And so, there were KLV camps all over Slovakia and the Czech Lands – and in Poland – everywhere. The children were there for years. They went home when their fathers returned from the war on leave, and they stayed home for fourteen days and then returned. These were average children. Their parents were happy that they didn't have to experience the constant bombings at night. There were also people who took their children out of school and brought them to relatives in small villages for school because they didn't want to participate in the school evacuation programme. But generally, everybody agreed to this. The children were spared a great deal of suffering and besides they were fed well. The schools were really big with 1,000 children. The teachers were required to go along – the men were especially happy to go because they didn't have to go to war and shoot at anybody or get killed themselves. They were required to do war service. But the camp leadership was in the hands of the Hitler Youth. There was a camp team leader for both the boys' and the girls' schools.

Behringer: Father (on the left) saluting Hitler in Coburg in 1936.

Behringer: Father's bother, sitting in the cabin of the truck on the far right (only head and shoulder can be seen) was a high-ranking SA officer in Coburg ca. 1925.

Bartmann: Serbia 1942, far right.

Burning synagogue in Bonn, 1938. (Courtesy of the City Archive and Historical Library of Bonn)

Losenhausen: Family photo, 1944.

Burned Jewish store in Bonn, 1938. (Courtesy of the City Archive and Historical Library of Bonn)

Okrajek: School photo.

Kamutzki.

Uphoff: Standing in the back row to the left together with staff at the Bergmannsheil Hospital in Bochum, 1944.

Destruction of Brüdergasse in Bonn, 1944. (Courtesy of the City Archive and Historical Library of Bonn)

Destruction of the Bonn Market Square, 1944. (Courtesy of the City Archive and Historical Library of Bonn)

Langenberg: Working for the Red Cross, 1945.

Jansen: Family photo.

Wiedenhammer.

Thomalla: On the upper right, with parents below. Her brother, on the left, died shortly afterwards as an artillery helper at the age of 16.

Ermer: 1933/34 with her father, a police officer, in Laasen near Sarau in the district of Schweidnitz.

Mirek: Wedding photo near the end of the war.

Schiffer: Junker Company, 1949.

Pfannenschmidt: Lazarette in Bordeaux, 1943 (top row, second from the left), complete Ear, Nose, Throat medical staff.

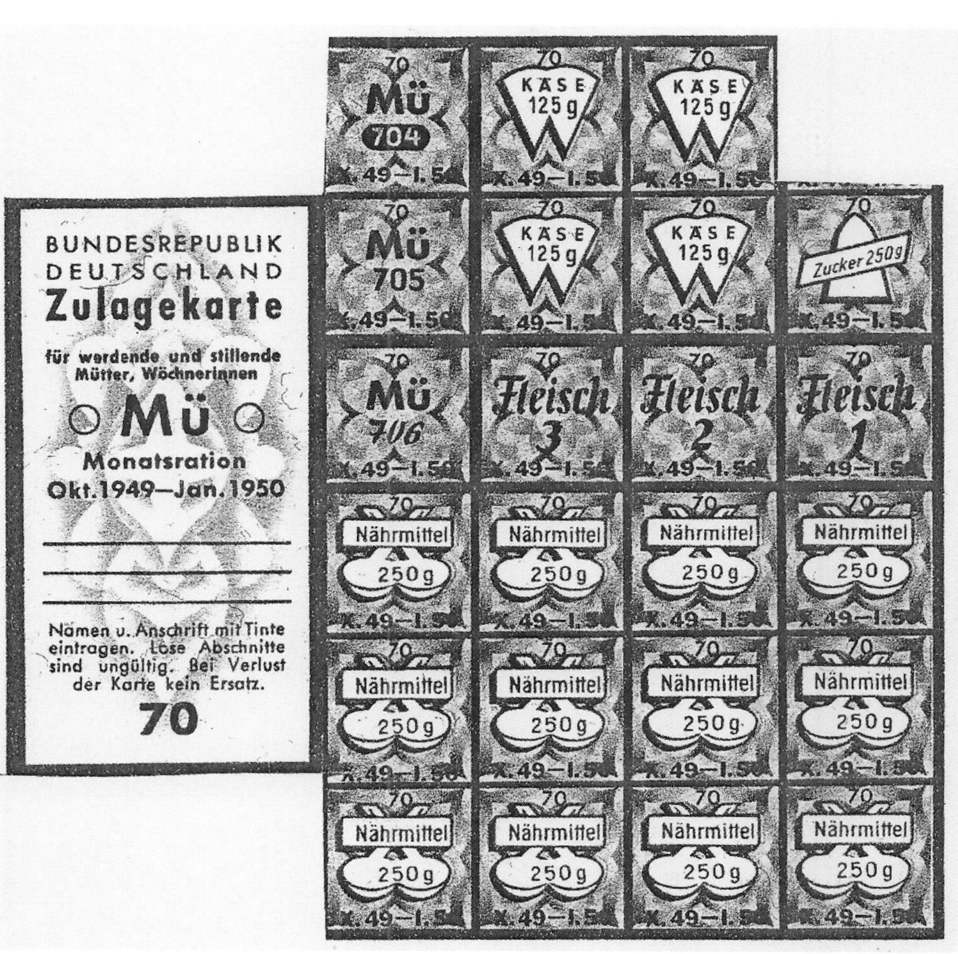

Emmel: Rations card.

Kahl: With husband and in-laws in Neuhaus on the Elbe at the end of the war.

What happened when the Allies came?

When the Allies were about to arrive, the camps were disbanded and the children were sent home as far as it was possible – also individually – and we of course had great difficulties – at that time there was Slovakia – and in Slovakia there was an uprising – and this was in the middle of Slovakia – and we already moved our camps to Vienna via Hungary – and from the middle of Slovakia the camps came to us in the Tatra Mountains – and we were there with them completely isolated and couldn't move either east or west. It was an unpleasant feeling. It was in August 1944. It was very unpleasant. I was outside on my birthday and heard the roaring of a truck. It was the SS. They had crossed the border from Katowice – normally nobody from the protectorate Bohemia and Moravia and from – what's it called again? – in Poland – normally nobody was allowed over the border. But the SS came with a big truck and loaded the 4,000 children onto it, drove us over the border, and placed us on a train to travel home.

Anneliese Radtke was born in Bonn in 1931. After her mother died at the beginning of the war, she was evacuated to Czechoslovakia with other children in 1942/43 to avoid the bombings in western Germany.

My mother died when I was 3 years old, and my father was left with four small girls. I was the youngest. He would have had to put us in an orphanage or send us to various relatives. My father was already terribly sad because they had a good marriage, and then, if his children had been taken away from him, that would have been the worst thing for him. At first, an old aunt took care of us, and later he married a young woman. But if you're so young and then you suddenly have such a large family – it's not the way it is today that you have everything like a washing machine. You had to cook on the stove and scrub the laundry, and everything was really primitive. You know? I never bonded with her because I always missed my mother. I was too small and looked for my mother my entire life. And that's why I've remained an individualist. I didn't mind being sent away for some recreation.

Children came together from the entire region: Cologne, Düren, Essen, and Bonn. You have to realize that there were constantly low-flying planes and bombing raids, and we spent more time in basements than in school or at home no matter whether it was day or night. We didn't have any peace and quiet anymore. It was terrible in Bonn. So, they evacuated the children to the country mostly so that they could rest and nothing would happen to them. And we found a place to stay in Spindlermühle in the district of Hohenelbe [in Sudetenland]. We were lucky. That's a ski area. The house we stayed in was a small hotel with nice beds. There were twenty-two of us girls of the same age. We had a camp director and a camp leader for girls. And the leader was also our teacher. She was kind-hearted and always came to our beds at night. She spoke with us and comforted us. Some of the children were homesick – the way it is in the beginning – and cried a lot. In the evenings there were songs on the piano, and we sang: "I want to walk back to Cologne." And then it was worse, and the mood reached a low point. But she often went hiking with us. And it was the first time that I was on Snow Mountain [Czech: Sněžka or Polish: Śnieżka]. It was rather foggy. And I thought: "My God, you can't see anything. No railing or anything." It was somehow eerie to go up there in the fog. When we were on the top between the clouds – and the sun was shining below – it was such a wonderful view. Since that time, I have loved the mountains. I used to go to the mountains in Oberstdorf in Oberallgäu every year. I was crazy about hiking and climbing in the mountains, but all of that is over now. In any case, we had a camp leader for girls, and she also went on hikes with us. You know the way it was in the Third Reich. The flag was taken down at night and raised again in the morning. We lifted our hands and sang a nice song. It was somehow fun. It didn't feel like it was punishment or anything. That was just a part of it. You know? And the story of Adolf Hitler. You forget about that years later. It disappeared from your mind.

They couldn't send us home. Our homes had been bombed out in the meantime. I had been there for more than half a year. The camp was about to be closed. They couldn't keep us forever. Right? The children had to be brought to their parents. And because we had been bombed out and were in the protectorate of Bohemia and Moravia at that time, we travelled to Bad Liebenwerda in 1943. It wasn't as nice there: there was a large room and double beds with sacks of straw. Before we had been spoiled with nice beds. We learned how to ski, but we had to share the skis because there were other groups that wanted to practise. They really made a great effort with us. I'd say that it was the best year of my youth. I really enjoyed it. Really. They made such an effort. I needed that. It was like a community. I didn't notice anything about the war. In the meantime, my stepmother had been evacuated to Silesia near Görlitz with my sisters. When our camp was closed in 1944, I had to go there. In the village school, all grades from the first to the eighth were in one classroom. We only had school sometimes, because we had to help the farmers in the fields during the harvest. At the end of 1944, the first refugees arrived from faraway places like West Prussia I believe, and the soldiers returned. There were a lot of White Russians. I had only heard about them. I couldn't recognize them as a child, and I also wasn't very interested. In any case, they all passed through for days and weeks. And we were the last ones. They said that we had to leave. In the distance you could hear the rolling thunder of the tanks and the shots.

And then we travelled through the snow for hours with a baby carriage, a cart, and suitcases. We went from one town to the next and had to leave everything behind. Otherwise, we wouldn't have been able to continue. And then the German armed forces came and took us along on trucks. And you weren't able to take anything along, just your bare life. And then we came to a train station somewhere, and they put us on a train. And we first found refuge in a church. We travelled back and forth by train and fled for four weeks. Do you know what it was like? The train was overcrowded. The Red Cross was standing at the train stations with tea and sandwiches. My sister, who always took care of us, jumped off the train quickly, afraid that it would drive off, and managed to get a few things for us. But my small brother, who was only 9 months old, died of hunger. We warmed up tea in a bottle with a candle. I can't explain to you how we managed to survive. In any case, after travelling endlessly back and forth with low-flying planes overhead, we arrived in Neumarkt in Oberpfalz. We had to get off the train and flee into the woods nearby because of the low-flying planes. When everything had settled down, they carried out the dead and my small brother. He had starved to death. I don't know whether they buried him or not. Probably. I don't know. In any case, there were elderly people who couldn't get anything to eat and had starved to death. And then we were in a gym for a few days, and they took care of us.

And then they said that we would be split up among the villages. My sisters were always a bit afraid and held on tightly to my stepmother and the other siblings. I was so independent and thought that it didn't matter where I was. It didn't matter whether I was in one village or another. I went to one village and came to a family with three children. We were all deadly ill because of dysentery. Once I recovered and started feeling better again, they said to me: "Now you have to go to the bread farmer." Each of them had a special name. One was the barber, and another was the bread farmer because he baked bread on his farm. I had to work like an adult. And I cried. I said: "I don't want to feed the pigs. I don't want to clean the pig stall." Nobody asked me. And nobody told me that I had to go to school. I was dumb. Nobody asked. I wasn't able to repeat the school year. When I went back home at Christmas in 1945, my father worked for the police in Bonn. He had to do homeland work since he hadn't been sent to the Front because of his children. And in the meantime, he had found a flat for us. And for that reason, we were able to return home exactly on Christmas Eve in 1945. And they said that there wasn't any work. I turned 14 and had to take care of the household. I said: "I don't want to." But it didn't matter, I had to do the housework. After half a year, I found a traineeship in a perfume and soap factory. I completed my traineeship and later got married.

Exodus from Silesia

Eva Maria Schmidt was born in Brunswick (Braunschweig) in 1924. She was sent to eastern Poland late in 1944 to perform her Reich Labour Service work and was forced to flee from the oncoming Russian Army.

I had to do my Reich Labour Service late in the war in 1944 because it had been postponed. It was in Poland in the easternmost camp that we had. It was in Warthegau – in Sockelstein. All of these places have different names today. Our train stopped in an open field. It was winter, and it was horrible. I then went to the camp for my labour service. The others there had to help out with work in the fields. In this place there were a lot of young women with small children who had been evacuated from Berlin. They lived there in order to be spared the bombings. I took care of the kindergarten. That was good for me because there were 100 kilograms of potatoes and 100 kilograms of red beets. We ate them alternately – once the potatoes and then the red beets. We didn't have anything else. And I could eat as much as I wanted from the potatoes and the red beets. You don't forget things like that once you've starved.

They told us that we couldn't leave the area because whoever did so was deserting. It was nonsense, but that's what they told us. They were storing some sort of material in the church – we didn't know what – we didn't go in there. And there were two soldiers who guarded it. They said that they would tell us when we had to leave the area. It became louder and louder, and we heard the sound of shooting from the Front. And we weren't allowed to leave. Crazy, wasn't it? We weren't allowed to leave. And then we noticed that the soldiers were long gone and that they didn't even tell us. And then we had to put on our best uniforms. Our private clothes, which we had worn to get there, had to be left in the barracks. We weren't allowed to take them along or wear them. We were in uniform and took along the remaining food that was there.

I'll never forget it: There was artificial honey and bread. Everyone had these things in their backpacks and also received new shoes. Everything that we had beforehand wasn't in good shape anymore. We even got new boots. We got new boots because it was winter, and we couldn't work outside in low-cut shoes. And there were Poles who were supposed to drive us to the train station by horse and carriage. You can't hold it against them. But they left all of us standing by the side of the road. You can't hold it against them. We didn't hold it against them. They were supposed to drive a few girls in uniform. And then we continued on foot and went to the train station. It was horrible: People in uniform from our camp and all the mothers were standing there with their children. And the shooting became louder and louder. And louder and louder. It was a horrible sound that I can't get out of my head anymore. And then a train came and someone jumped off and said: "You can't leave the girls in uniform here. The next train is the Russians." It was clear what he meant. The Russians treated women horribly, you know. And that's no tale. But you probably have heard that from many people who experienced it.

Did you see it yourself?

No, but we believed what others told us. And then someone said: "What are they supposed to do? Sit down between us. We're on our way back from the Front." Several injured soldiers were being transported and it was horrible for us. "Don't bother the doctors and nurses. Sit down somewhere. Do you have anything to eat? You have to give us everything, or we won't take you along." Of course, we gave them everything. And then we were out of there. And then we still hadn't been released from service. We were brought to three different camps. And then we were brought to the barracks in a fourth camp and slept on the bare floor without blankets or anything. But we also had a coat which was part of our uniform. It wasn't thick, but it was nice and warm. And then there was a diphtheria epidemic, and we weren't allowed to leave the barracks anymore. They placed food in front of the door. The women's camp was near Berlin, and then one day, around Christmas time, they told us that we should go home because they couldn't help us anymore. We had to get home on our own while in uniform. I somehow managed to do it.

You do a lot of things although you're not totally fit. And I made it to Brunswick. I found my mother and my sister again. My father hadn't yet returned from the war.

Well, I don't know how they knew it, but some people told us that we were very lucky because the Americans were coming and not the Russians. All the women were afraid of the Russians. And that was no tale. It was really like that. The Americans were coming. And I know that we were still starving and heard that the rations depot from the German armed forces had been pillaged. My sister, my girlfriend, and I went there by bike over the fields and took a big cardboard box full of canned sausage. And then we pounced on it and were so sick afterwards. We hadn't eaten fat and meat and things like that for such a long time.

We were riding our bikes back from the depot, and suddenly we were astounded and shocked. A tank with American soldiers was approaching us on the road. In the front of the tank there were – today you're not allowed to say the word anymore – Negroes. And we had never seen a Negro before in our entire lives. We stood there with our bicycles and didn't know whether we should throw away the boxes – but the precious meat – we couldn't toss the cans onto the fields. We wanted to take it along. And then the Americans came to us, and we trembled. And what did they do? They threw chocolate and oranges to us and kept on calling out: "Hello, blondie. Hello, blondie!" My sister and I used to be so blonde, almost white-blonde. We gathered all those things together onto our bicycles and quickly rode home over the stubble-fields. The Americans were there first, but we didn't notice them much. Afterwards, the English arrived. And I can't say it in any other way – and I'm not saying it because of you – they were incredibly nice to us: the Americans as well as the English. They were nice to us girls, to my mother, and to the rest of the population. We were in basements in bombed-out buildings or somewhere else with six or eight people housed in one room. We didn't have anything to eat. And they were all very nice. And suddenly the war was over.

Crossing the Baltic Sea

Hella Weidenhammer was born in Meldorf in Schleswig-Holstein. She recalls the evacuation of Danzig by ship at the end of 1944 and the fate of the *Wilhelm Gustloff*.

What was your reason for going to Danzig?

My fiancé was there. My sister had a student flat, and I was able to stay with her there in the beginning. And then I went to city hall and said: "Here I am. And these are my credentials. Which job do you have for me?" And I was lucky. There was a position available as the head of a childcare centre in Brösen – that was a small fishing village between Danzig and Zoppot – which also included a partially furnished two-room flat. That was just the right thing for me. I was still very young and didn't have any work experience. I had to really think about whether I was able to do the work. There were sixty children who had to be looked after every day and nine employees in the centre. I was 21 years old. And it wasn't so easy. But it was a great deal of fun. And we got married in Danzig. Back then it wasn't usual that all your friends came to the wedding. That was impossible. And still, we managed – we got married. I had my job in the childcare centre, and my husband was a research assistant at the Torpedo Experimentation Institute in Gotenhafen. They worked on acoustic target-searching torpedoes.

During Christmas 1944, we noticed that the Front was very close. For example, at night we saw the smoke from Marienburg and heard shooting. And, since we had this childcare centre, there were a lot of available beds and sanitary facilities such as showers and so on. Beginning in November 1944, soldiers started coming to the childcare centre to rest for the weekend. They brought their own food, and I only had to provide them with a room with these small beds and sanitary facilities. We would greet them and say: "How are you? You're here again?"

Were they on their way home from the Front?

No, they weren't on their way home. They were on leave for a weekend during the war so that they could rest. And then they had to go back. Marienburg is not far from Danzig. That was a few weeks before the end of the war so we wondered how we would get away from there. We were also responsible for the children who had been brought there. It was a childcare centre, and the children lived at home, but in spite of that we took care of them during the day while their parents were working. You had to really think about whether you wanted to leave. But my husband received a ticket for the ship – you didn't have any telephone back then – even in companies – today I can't imagine how it was possible – and we sent one another telegrams. And then I knew that he had the ticket, and I had to travel to Gotenhafen so that I could also leave. And I simply took along that which I could carry. I knew what you needed when your house was bombed such as cooking pots and silverware and thread – and a lot of things that you normally don't think about. My house had already been bombed before. I packed all of these things together and went to Gotenhafen. It was bitter cold that winter with snow storms so that you sometimes thought to yourself: "Just stay here and sit for a while." That's how unpleasant the weather was.

And then I got my ticket for the *Hansa*, and my acquaintance wanted to travel together with me. Then we were on the *Hansa* – not only were all of the cabins filled – but in every room people were on the sofas and some on the floors – there were 2,000 people on board. Only civilians. Maybe a few injured soldiers, but the ship was for civilians. And the situation was such that the *Hansa* didn't leave and the *Gustloff* had already departed. And we thought to ourselves: "Why doesn't it leave?" And then they didn't turn on the radio anymore so that we didn't know anything at all. And we didn't get any answers to our questions. "Why don't we depart?" All of us would have liked to go back home again and take more of what we had left behind. But no one was allowed to leave the ship, and we waited for two days. We weren't supposed to sail behind the *Gustloff* which just sank.[1] And we weren't supposed to know that it sank so that there would be no panic. And we didn't know that the *Gustloff* sank until we were almost in Kiel. They knew how to manage that. First of all, people were obedient and didn't ask many questions.

And they knew how to suppress these kinds of things. The *Gustloff* was torpedoed by a Russian submarine just after it departed. During the war they didn't ask whether it was a passenger ship or not. It didn't matter.

Did you know people on the *Gustloff*?

Yes, many. Even with babies. Well, once the *Gustloff* departed we travelled along the coast, and that's why it took so long – they were very careful. And on board everyone was actually very disciplined. They wanted to get away and didn't have any other thoughts. They were sleeping on the floors and in armchairs in the cabins. For example, I was in a two-bed interior cabin. There were four of us with a baby. But it was alright. It was alright. That's because we were so obsessed with the idea that we had to leave there and that it just had to work.

And when we arrived in Kiel, it was so well organized that we got onto a bus and were brought to a gymnasium hall somewhere. We got something to eat there. There was a corner where men slept, and another where women slept in the hall. On the next morning, we were supposed to be brought to farms or other places. And my acquaintance and I didn't want that. We wanted to go to Hamburg because we had family there. At night we secretly climbed out of the window – we first threw our suitcases out of the window – but we didn't know the town we were in. On the following morning, we noticed that people were going in the direction of the train station, or in a certain direction, so we went along with them with our suitcases. It was actually a small train station, but I can't recall the name of the town. And from there we went to Hamburg, and each of us went to our families in Hamburg. I went to my in-laws who were surprised to see me.

Helene Campers was born in Königsberg in East Prussia in 1914. She recalls her flight across the Baltic Sea from the oncoming Russian forces.

In the spring of 1944, we noticed that the Russians were coming closer and closer. My sister had to flee earlier and came by sea because the

Russians had cut off retreat by land. She was one of the last to leave Königsberg by ship and came to me in Pomerania. They were allowed to evacuate the orphanage because the district party leader had permitted it. And then they smuggled us in – my children, me, my sister, and my mother. We took care of the children. And then we travelled by ship from Pomerania to Mecklenburg – the eastern part of Mecklenburg. As we sailed, there were shipwrecks on our right and left – one after the other. There were a horrible number of people packed onto the ship. It was so full, and people were frightened that they wouldn't have enough room to lie down to sleep. Do you know what I did? I brought together my children and all the children from the orphanage and sang simple songs with them – children's songs and hymns – in their children's voices. And these songs alone calmed everyone down. And suddenly everyone had the feeling that there was enough room – that there was room for everyone. It was only the fear that they didn't have enough room which made everyone aggressive. Children's songs – music and art – have great power in times like these. I was able to sing well and knew a lot of children's songs – I was talented in this respect – and the children's voices calmed everyone down. And we saw the shipwrecks on our right and left, and our ship continued on. I don't know who steered it. I think it was God's power and spirit – which we needed so much and which saved us.

Elisabeth Neff recalls leaving Stolp in Eastern Pomerania and crossing the Baltic Sea on *Bore VI* to escape the advancing Russian forces.

I left on 6 March and arrived in Danzig on 8 March 1945. We went out backwards. Here is Stolp – and we went east because we couldn't go west. The Russians came across the bottom and circled the region so that we couldn't go west. So, we went backwards to Danzig – to a port right before Danzig called Saspe. There we boarded a ship – it wasn't a passenger ship, but rather a cargo ship. At first, there was a low wooden barrier on board with bags of straw around it, but that wasn't any use. Once we were on board, passengers stormed the ship so that we almost sank because it was so full. We set sail so that no one else could get on board. And everything was organised. We were young women between the ages of 20 and 30, and they prepared a small room in the front of the ship for us to lie down. It was cold because we were at sea in March, so they brought in potbelly stoves. The pipes of the stove were at least 10 metres tall, and there was a hatch with a hole. Once or twice a day, the hatch opened up so that air could enter. I personally was not so adventurous, but I met a girl who said: "We're not staying here. Let's put on some warm clothes and go on deck." And there were crew members, and she started to flirt with them. That was good because she told them that we wanted to stay on duty with them. And we did. Then we were allowed to drink a cup of hot coffee. Then she also asked them if we could all – there were eight or ten of us girls – wash ourselves in the engine room. We were at sea for so long. We set sail on March 10 and were on the Baltic Sea at this time and first arrived on 21 March. We had waited a long time for an accompanying ship because the *Gustloff* had sunk earlier. We had waited a long time and were wearing a lot of clothes because it was cold. And we felt dirty. She said to them that each of us wanted a bucket of warm water. And she said: "Don't look. Hang up a curtain or go away." And they did. We went down there with four girls – and then four more girls – and we were able to really wash ourselves. That was nice. In this way, we felt fresh again. It was good for me because I didn't have to stay in that stinky room – but I still had to sleep there. That was clear. At night we went there. And you could hear how people were vomiting when the ship rocked. I was able to go out frequently and that was pleasant. We travelled as far as Warnemünde and Rostock and then by freight train to Güstrow.

Oh, yes. I have to tell you who I was travelling with. I forgot that. My sister was a civil employee at the Stolp-Reitz Airfield. I was sitting in my office, and she came to me on 6 March and said: "The entire military airfield is being moved to Lübeck. And we are allowed to take along one family member." Otherwise, the employees would have had to travel alone. And I had an acquaintance in the west and was interested in going along. And I said: "Take care of everything that needs to be done. I'll go home." My boss immediately said: "Go ahead." I packed all my things together at home. My mother cooked, but I wasn't hungry.

I just cried the whole time. And, of course, we weren't able to carry our suitcases. So, my father put the two suitcases on a small transport wagon and brought us through the entire city. And they took the luggage from there. They helped us onto a freight train so that we were able to go to Danzig. Otherwise, we wouldn't have been able to travel there. That's what I forgot to mention.

Hiding from the Russians

Maria Thomalla was born in Oberglogau in Upper Silesia in 1930. At the age of 14, she fled with her mother from the advance of the Red Army.

It was precisely on 19 January 1945 during the night when an air-raid warden came to us and said that it was the end of the line and the last train was leaving. He told us that either we go along or horrible things would happen to us. The soldiers had already left, and you could hear the thunder of artillery and cracking of guns everywhere. We had known fourteen days in advance that the trains were ready for transport and that some of us were supposed to leave the area. We thought that we would return again after the Russians had been driven back. Three quarters of the people left the city in special trains. And over and over again my mother refused to leave because my brother worked as an artillery helper nearby. She didn't want to leave him alone. But then the shooting became louder and louder, and we said: "Mother, let's go."

My mother tidied up our house and cleaned everything and made everything look nice after Christmas. And she left behind a few things for my brother in case he came back. She assumed that it would only be for a short period of time and then some miracle would happen. She always believed in miracles. Then she took the sledge out and placed me on it. I didn't want her to do that because I wanted to pull her. It was a cold winter night, and there was a lot of snow. So, I had to sit on the sledge with a small suitcase and a small bag. I was 14 years old. And then we groped along in the dark on our way to the train station. Nobody was outside, and it was completely dark. Everything had to be dark because of the air-raid sirens. Nobody was around. And then we came to the train station, and there was a long train that was half filled. There were nurses from the Red Cross, and we sat down there. The train didn't have any windows anymore. And we waited and waited for it to leave. And then finally it left. And, because of the bombings, we had to take another route. And then suddenly we stopped, and someone shouted that everyone had to get out of the train. An airplane flew overhead and shot at the train with a machine gun. And then it flew away, and we got back onto the train. There are horrible stories: A mother was holding her dead child and didn't want to give it up. They took the child away from her and threw it out the window. And then we travelled for a while, and suddenly they said that it was the end of the line. We had to walk the rest of the way. We got out of the train, took the sledge again, and got onto a road. German soldiers were going past who were also retreating. We asked them if we could drive along with them for a while because my grandmother lived nearby. That's where we wanted to go. It was near Oberglogau. They were really nice guys and loaded us onto a truck and took us along for a while. And shortly before Oberglogau, we got off again and went to my grandparents'.

The situation was horrible there: A young woman had just died, and my grandmother was left alone with three small children on the farm. And the Polish farmhands were a little aggressive. She was really lost there. And it was the end of the line, and we had to stay there. We waited there a while because we also didn't know what we were supposed to do. Grandmother couldn't leave. The shooting practically followed us so we knew that the end was near. Everything was moving in the direction of the west. And then they [the Russians] formed a ring around Oppeln, Oberglogau, and Gleiwitz and nothing came in or out anymore. And one night there was a horrible thundering sound of artillery and tank guns and things like that. And an SS unit came and broke through this ring and left part of it open and got out all the refugees. But, as I said, we had to stay there because of the small children. And then the SS also withdrew and had very little understanding for the fact that my mother remained there with me. Mother told them that this was the only way. Then they withdrew, and we waited until the Russians arrived. That happened two days later.

First the tanks came, and they just drove past. They didn't take any notice of us. And then the small carriages came with Asians. They first threw us out of our homes and told us that we should disappear. And we went to another village. We were thrown out again. And then we went back to our houses, and when we arrived some SS soldiers were being held on the neighbour's farm. They caught around fifty of them and kept them at the neighbour's farm house. Later I found out that these were guys who didn't voluntarily join the SS. They went to schools and asked who wanted to join the SS. When nobody raised their hands, they told them to count off. And the number ones went to the regular army, and the number twos to the SS. These guys were all 20 to 25 years old. And the Russians stood all of them up against the wall and shot them. And we had to bury them and then work.

But before the Russians arrived, the people in the village hid all of us young girls in a hole under the barn. We were crouched down there, and we heard shooting and more shooting. We thought that no one was alive anymore, and we had to look outside. Nobody wanted to go, and finally I said: "Okay, I'll go." I went out with another girl into the village. There were bonfires everywhere, and it was so dark. And we went into Grandmother's house. All the grandmothers, who had made themselves look old, were sitting around a round table: A young Russian was telling them about how he was a decent guy and would never bother any woman and so on. And we went inside, and he stood up and said: "Come along! Come along immediately!" He pressed his machine gun against our backs and pushed us outside. And my mother ran behind him: "You can't do that!" He didn't understand her. And we were outside at the beginning of the street. And my mother spoke with another Russian soldier who had a somewhat higher rank, a sergeant or something like that, and she argued with him and pulled him towards us. And then there was a dispute, and my mother said to us: "Run away!" And we ran down the village road. Naturally, they turned around and shot at us immediately. One of the shots breezed through my hair. Another one hit a post near me. And others flew by me here and there. We ran back into the barn and found the hole again. My mother ran behind us and shouted: "Are you inside? Are you inside?" The other girls held my mouth so that I couldn't answer her. But I answered her. Her voice sounded so desperate. I said: "Yes, Mother, we're in here." And then the great search began. They poked around with poles and everything possible to find the hole. And for some reason they couldn't find it. We stayed in the hole for three or four days, and then mother got us out because these guys had moved on.

And then new Russians came, and we had to work. For example, I had to sew button holes. And the others had to sew or whatever. But we no longer lived in our house. We weren't allowed back there anymore. The Russians came precisely on 19 March 1945. I left Beuthen on 19 January, and the first Russians came on 19 March. And in May it gradually became warmer, and we had to work in the fields and gather the dead Russians. Of course, they were in awful shape. And we did this without any gloves. We gathered them together, but I don't know what they did with them. They were brought to a war veterans' cemetery somewhere.

CHAPTER IV

THE RUSSIAN INVASION

Silesia

Gisela Ermer was born in Zauditz in the district of Ratibor in Upper Silesia in 1921. While her husband was recovering in a military hospital in Bavaria, the Russian military command occupied her house in 1945 in the town of Habelschwerdt in the county of Glatz.

The Russians came and made a reasonable impression during the day. We had our own house, and it was nicely furnished. Of course, they liked it. And one guy said: "This is where the commander is going to stay." They were wearing green caps. But did I know what green caps meant? It was the secret police. I didn't have any idea. And my parents who didn't live far from me said: "You can't stay there if Russians are inside." I answered: "I can't leave the house alone when the Russians are there. It's impossible. I have to stay there." During the day, the commander responsible for the troops over our whole street was very nice. And I was supposed to cook dinner or something for him to eat – it was no problem. But he drank vodka at night and that was not so pleasant. I wondered that he wanted the room where my daughter slept. It was such a tiny room. It wasn't our master bedroom.

And earlier, when I went to town, I met a young woman with a baby in a carriage, and she was crying. And I said to her: "What's wrong? Why are you crying?" The Russians were not there yet. It was one or two days beforehand. "Oh", she said, "we're from the west. We were brought here because they aren't dropping bombs here. I delivered my baby here. And the child has to be bathed. It needs something to eat. I don't know where I should go." I said to her: "You know, I have a room for you. I don't have a baby bath, but I do have a bath tub. It doesn't have to be a baby bath. And we'll be able to find some milk for the baby." And then I took the woman along, and she was in my house. And, as I said, the Russians came. During the day everything was fine, and, in the evening, I made dinner. And then I took my daughter with me, and we went upstairs and withdrew to our room. And I locked the door. It was fine for a while, but then he came to our door and wanted to come inside. And I knew that we couldn't hold the door shut for long if a man used his full strength against it. Our daughter was 12 or 13 years old at that time. And she said: "What are we going to do?" I said: "You know what we are going to do, Renate? We'll make him look foolish. Go to the window and shout for help. And I'll stay at the door and try to prevent him from kicking it in." And we did that. And he wasn't able to do anything to us if he didn't want to embarrass himself as the leader of his troops. The plan was good. But I didn't reckon with the woman with the baby who lived in the room next door. She needed milk for the baby and opened the door. I told her to close the door and to keep it shut. And then I thought to myself: "What are you going to do? You have to help her. You can't leave her alone." I was forced to open my door. That was a risky situation.

The woman had gone somewhere with the baby, and he grabbed hold of my daughter and wanted to drag her into the room. And I pulled her away from him, put her behind me, and walked backwards to the top of the stairs that led to the door. I said, "Run fast to grandma", because she didn't live far away. But now I was still there. And the rage in the man came to a boil. It was understandable. He drew his pistol. Since my father had worked for the police, I knew when a weapon was secured and when it wasn't secured. And I saw that he had released the lock. Even if he hadn't wanted to shoot – and simply made an uncontrollable movement – he would have shot even if he hadn't wanted to. He was drunk at that moment. And then he approached me with this unlocked weapon – very closely – I was on the top of the stairs and had to either go down or ... He aimed his weapon at me; his pistol wasn't locked anymore. People say that your entire life passes before your eyes. I didn't have that much time. There was such tension inside of me – I wanted to get rid of this tension – so that I thought: "My God!" And I probably shouted out loud because I was so afraid. "Shoot, will you?" I thought that it was over. And because of the loud shouting he came to his senses, took the pistol, locked it again, and threw it into the corner behind him.

"What's going to happen now?" I wondered. I thought that my only chance was to run away. And I did. I ran down the stairs, and at the bottom was my daughter. “What are you doing here?” I asked. “I thought that you were at Grandma’s house.” She said: “I was so afraid for you.” Oh, my God. That was my daughter, and she was afraid for me. She had heard everything. I thought: “Let’s leave everything here. They can destroy it and trample on it. It doesn’t matter. Go to your parents’ house.” I wanted to go outside, but there was a guard there with a bayonet pointed towards me. He was the boss. I didn’t count on seeing him. We had called for help, and he wondered if something had happened. Nothing had happened to us. But the man couldn’t have known that. And I thought that we had to get past him. You can behave like a wild child so that he would think that strange things happened that night. I had to put on an act. I put the child behind me, and we were off to my parents’ house.

Early the next morning my father brought us to an electronics workshop. There were large basement rooms, and we hid there with blankets and everything that we had taken from my parents’ house. We stayed there and were safe, so to speak. But this Russian was looking for us everywhere on the streets. He went through all the houses and looked for us, but couldn’t find us. And then he tried to demolish everything in our house that he could find. My husband’s very valuable stamp collection was burned. Things like that. Canning jars were in the backyard – it was horrible. And the landing of the staircase was covered in thick jam. He did things like this because he was so angry. But we were safe – nothing else was important. I know that he went through all the houses and couldn’t find us. Then they went on – they were forced to move on. And I returned to my ravaged house.

Western Pomerania

Helene Krüger was born in 1927 in Menthen in West Prussia in the district of Stuhm near Marienburg. She recalls the atrocities committed by Russian soldiers during the invasion of Germany.

I had to leave my Catholic girls' school and perform my Reich Labour Service for one year. The work was alright. We had to help rich families who had school children. I only did this work for a quarter of a year – that was in the autumn. What really surprised me was that they sent young girls in the direction of the Front. The Russians were coming closer and closer. And we were going in the direction of the Russians – we were being sent towards the Russians. Our camp was always right next to the Front. We heard the thundering. One morning, I woke up and was alone at the camp. I will never forget it: I must have been in such a deep sleep, and they disappeared. They left in different directions, but I can't say where they went. I got up, looked around, was afraid, and looked around some more. I tried to find people. Then I went to the train station. Now and then a train left. Those were trains with open cars – not passenger trains. I was lucky because I was able to jump onto one of the cars with my backpack and took the train to northern Germany, first to Stettin. From there I travelled in the direction of northern Germany to Peenemünde near Stralsund.

I then went to a family. I was alone. The father of the family was looking for workers, but I didn't know anything about work yet. They needed workers, and I went along. [laughs] I didn't know what was expected of me. In any case, I experienced the Russian invasion together with this family. The Russians came closer and closer. That was in January, February, and March 1945. I thought that the Russians would leave us alone. I always had the pleasure of being near the Russians! Anyway, when the Russians entered the village and their artillery fire blasted, we thought that we would be safe from the Russians on the farm. And what happened? We went there with the family without the father. He stayed at home. He must have been ill; otherwise, he would have been a soldier. They wouldn't have allowed anyone to stay at home. In any case, the door suddenly opened, and a Russian was standing in the doorway. He wanted to have a woman to rape. We were sitting there, and he came running towards me and tried to grab hold of me. I started to scream and cry! Then he said: "Don't cry. Don't cry", and looked around for another woman. I had just turned 18 – it must have been in April or May when the Russians came. "Don't cry. Don't cry", he said. In any event, I'll never forget that he had such a large head. I guess that he must have been a Mongolian. I vaguely remember him taking hold of the farmer's wife and bringing her to the cow stable. And he raped the farmer's wife; otherwise, it would have been me. Afterwards, we went back to the village because it was even less safe on the farm than in the city. They didn't bomb the city – only shot off their weapons. We had a hiding spot in the hay. We lay down flat and the shots passed over our heads. I don't know – when you're young you don't think about things like that. You think entirely differently. I wasn't afraid for my life, and I didn't wonder when it would be over – I can't claim that I was terribly afraid. I don't know why.

After a while it became quieter again. It was said about the Russian commander that he had a horrible venereal disease and wanted to infect as many German women as possible. That was the goal of the Russians. As I said, you had to watch out for the Russians. That's the reason why we hid from the Russians and the commander so that they wouldn't come and get us. Once they came to get you – either you were shot dead or you did what they wanted. But I was always lucky. I used to say that I had a guardian angel over my shoulder. In spite of everything that happened – I was still very lucky that I wasn't raped. The Russians gathered together youths – boys and girls who were 14 and 15 years old – and they beat the boys more than the girls. They told them that they had stayed at home and could have been soldiers and asked them why they were together with the girls at home. The Russian soldiers didn't get any vacation – any home leave – for the entire war. That's why they chased after young women. It was horrible. I can't even describe it to you. Everything was so unbelievable. And then we were dirty. You couldn't even really wash or change your clothes. We were really dirty animals. But, as I said, when you're young you put up with everything. We still had to hide even after they had been there for a while. As soon as you showed your face on the streets, the Russians grabbed hold of you.

Later I had to work together with the Russians. Among others, there was a female Russian soldier. She was so nice and always protected me. She said that she wasn't my enemy and protected me. If the Russians were bothersome – and they continued to come – she always stood behind me like a guardian angel. I will never forget how much I liked this woman. One day, they all withdrew and marched to the village. We then had to do factory work with heavy concrete and carry iron, and whoever didn't want to, or couldn't, was hit with the butt of the rifle. Afterwards, our private lives slowly started again. I cannot describe it all in detail. The experiences were so different. What was especially significant was that I didn't have a father or mother. My father died in the war, and my mother was on the road with my brothers and sisters. She had been detained by the Poles who behaved even worse than the Germans – than the Russians – maybe like the Germans in Russia, too. We don't know. People say that they behaved well there. There are episodes which cannot be described in detail. In any case, it was always difficult for a young girl to move about. I had an aunt in Berlin and was lucky that I went there later because the Russians took one of the rooms in her house and brought women there to rape them without any consideration of the consequences. By the time I went there, everything had quietened down.

How long did the Russians rape women?

One to two years. I had to work for the Russians and rented a room from an old woman. And when I met a Russian on my way home, I had to fight very energetically. Otherwise – we were only wild game for them. Stalin said that German women belonged to the Russian soldiers. And that's what they did. And not too seldom.

Königsberg

Manfret Schink was born in Königsberg in East Prussia in 1935. He recalls the occupation of the city by Russian soldiers in 1945 and being sent to an orphanage as a 10-year-old boy after his mother was killed while clearing mines and his father was taken prisoner by the Russians.

In April 1945 the commander of our home guard told us to go home because the Russians were coming. Our homes had already been bombed and destroyed. We went in the direction of Königsberg although our homes had been devastated. But I knew that my mother and grandmother were living in our bombed-out basement. My maternal grandmother had already left with my sister for Denmark and was in safety. When we came around the corner of a street in the city we heard shooting – they were still fighting at this time – and we saw soldiers standing there. I said to my friend Karl-Heinz Fischer – I'll never forget his name because he was my neighbour: "Hey, there are soldiers over there. Let's go and see." When we went there, they spoke to us in Russian. There was a Russian lieutenant – and I'll never forget – he looked at the two of us – we were wearing filthy military uniforms – and tears rolled down his face and he said: "Fucking Hitler." At that time, I didn't understand what he meant. Afterwards, I asked myself why he had tears in his eyes. It was probably frustration and the stress of the situation.

I then went into the basement to my mother. My father came afterwards. Thank God. He was stationed at the airport in Tegel as part of the ground personnel – he had also flown. Then we were forced to leave the basement. Although we were young boys, we saw how men and women fit together. The Russians didn't take us into consideration. Those were the combat troops who entered the city and were extremely brutal and pillaged and took women. As a 10-year-old boy I knew that there were men and women, but not what they did together. Today children are a lot cleverer. They forced us through Königsberg in the direction of the promenade. When we passed Königsberg Castle, there were German soldiers there who had already surrendered. SS units were still fighting in the castle. We saw the fighting with our own eyes. They brought us to the promenade to an open area. Many refugees were there. My father was taken away for an interrogation and never came back again. They took him away, and we were then alone. From the promenade they brought us to a hotel. The Russians took the women with them even if the women didn't go voluntarily. They didn't care if the children were sleeping next to them or not.

In order to get some bread and something to eat – which was extremely hard to find – the women got long sticks with a nail at the end and a pair of pliers from the Russians. They went through the fields in rows of five or seven women. When they noticed that the ground was hard, they slowly crouched down and cut the wire. The mines had a wire that had to be cut. As young boys we went along through the fields. My mother stepped on a mine. I saw my mother practically going up to heaven. There was no funeral. Nothing. I then wandered around on my own – slept in ruins – slept in the woods together with other boys – and then in mid-1946 they caught me stealing and sent me to an orphanage with German nuns.

The nuns did an outstanding job and worked together with the camp commander to provide for us. One day a Russian vehicle appeared before the orphanage, and my father climbed out and entered the building. He found out through others that I must have been at that orphanage ... He first brought me to his sister in Königsberg, who was living in a bombed-out basement, and came by to pick me up there later.

Berlin

Erni Mirek was born in Storkow in Brandenburg in 1919. She recalls giving birth to twins near Berlin at the end of the war while German women were being raped on the streets and houses pillaged by Russian soldiers.

We were suddenly told that the Russians were coming. "You have to leave! You have to leave! You have to leave!" We didn't hear anything from my father – he had been drafted in the war as – what do you call those old soldiers who were drafted at the end of the war? – old fighters. He had to dig ditches and fortify everything. A vehicle filled with Armed SS soldiers came to us and asked: "Do you want to stay here?" They went into every house – that's what acquaintances told me. "You have to leave here! You have to leave here! The Russians are coming. They are not far from here." The Russians were already in Frankfurt on the Oder. And we went along with the SS soldiers.[1]

How were the soldiers from the Armed SS?

Wonderful. Very accommodating. They asked: "Do you want to stay here or not – with your child and sister and mother?" My father wasn't there because he had been drafted. We first went along with them, and several families had already been on the large truck. They took along everyone they could find. Then they said: "More trucks are coming. Get ready and they'll pick you up." We left with the first truck. Our suitcases had already been packed because of the constant bombings, and I said to mother: "Come on – there's no sense in waiting – let's go along with them." My sister, my mother, my daughter, and I – the four of us – went along with the Armed SS. I don't know where they brought us – to some woods – and suddenly we stopped moving. And the SS soldiers got down from the truck and advanced forward. "Stay here, stay here", they said. "You can't go up front. We have to see how to get out of here." And the bombs started to fall, and we lay on the ground and nothing happened. I remember that there was a hole in the ground that had been dug – German soldiers, older men were down inside. One man from the SS soldiers came – I'll never forget it – and he took his rifle and said: "Either you let the women and children inside, or I'll shoot each of you." Then they made room for us, and we were able to go into the hole. It was a rather big hole. We all fit inside. And there was another family inside. No, it was a woman and a child – not an entire family. And we lay down there. I have to say that the Armed SS saved my life. One of them came back to see whether we were really inside the hole. I'm not sure where the older men went. My God, they were old and afraid just like us. Oh, I forgot to mention that I was pregnant.

I was pregnant. Imagine that. At first, I didn't want to go along with them, but then I thought: "You can't stay here!" The sky was full and already red when I looked up. That's why I said: "Mom, I'm going along." She said: "I won't leave you alone." So, we went together with my sister – I had a younger sister. Yes, and what happened then? The SS soldiers came back and saw that we were inside the hole, and the older men went along with them. I don't know where they stayed. Oh, yes, suddenly it [the bombing] stopped. We didn't hear anything anymore. And we didn't see any Germans anymore. And then two Russians came – you can imagine what we were thinking. But they didn't do anything to us three women or to the others. They only said: "O.K., start on your way home." One of them knew German well. I assume that he was from the Ukraine or whatever it's called. And he said: "Here are two horses and a wagon. There are two or three wounded soldiers lying on it. Take them along and drive home. Keep on going in this direction." And he showed us the way. A man first drove the wagon and then he said: "We have to switch places because I'm also injured." He had a leg injury. The Russian told us: "Stop at the next hospital and bring the injured soldiers inside." It was a long wagon. I had never seen a German wagon like that before. It was called a "panjewagon".[2] I sat in the front, and the others were in the back. We had blankets and so on. We were supposed to drop off the injured soldiers wherever there was room. If there wasn't room, we had to ask where the next hospital was. The Russians were very nice I have to say. They gave us the wagon – but could also have taken us with them. But they didn't do that.

Did the Russians allow you to take along the soldiers from the Armed SS to the next hospital?

No, they took along the Armed SS soldiers. They were gone. We didn't see any Armed SS soldiers anymore. The wounded soldiers were regular German soldiers. They must have been drafted because they were all older men. There weren't any young soldiers. That's what I meant by that. One of them knew his way around Berlin better than I did. I grew up in the woods. Where was I supposed to go? I didn't know Berlin at all. It was all wooded areas. One soldier said that the Russians explained to him that we had to go here or there. It must have been an interpreter who explained it to him. And he knew where to go. We went to each hospital to drop off patients, but we always got new ones to take along. And we didn't know where to go. Imagine that. And then how did we get home? I lived in a small town where there was an ammunition depot – that's the last place where we lived. We arrived there safely with two small horses and a long, long wagon. And no one was on it except for my family – my mother, my sister, and I – and I drove the wagon – and my small daughter – she was 4 years old. She always said: "Mommy, what mis-e-ry." She wasn't able to pronounce "misery" because she was too small. "Mis-e-ry." She always heard it from my mother who said: "What a misery this war is in our country. Oh, it's horrible!" And then we arrived home safely, but we saw that our house was not intact. There was a large hole in the roof. A grenade or something had landed on it. The Russians discovered the ammunition depot and bombed it terribly.

And then the misery began with the raping. That was the worst thing that you could experience as a woman. But I can thank the dear Lord. I spent over six weeks sleeping on the hay rafters of a barn. My father used to help the farmer's wife in the village – to bring in the harvest, and so on. My mother and I, and small Karin whom we always took along in the fields, also helped with the harvest. And then it started with the raping by the Russians. I wasn't able to stay at home: the door was crashed in and the windows were broken. Well, what was I supposed to do? My father wasn't back yet – he came later. And the farmer's wife had helped us where we and my father had worked. She said: "Come to me. I have the big barn and you can spend the night there. Rape is horrible." As soon as it turned dark, the Russians were outside. "Where are the women?" they asked. And they raped everyone in the village except for six women who were together on the hay rafters. And one of my acquaintances didn't want to be raped, and the Russians shot her on the spot. I can tell you truthfully. My sister said that she could have saved her own life. But she fought back so much that they shot her on the spot. It was in the middle of the day with three Russians. And they came back every night! And the six of us – we were all young women approximately my age – and there was a high ladder – oh, yes, my father returned home in the meantime. And he arranged for us to climb up to the rafters and stacked the hay up high so that no one could see anything. The Russians really couldn't find us up there. It would have been a stroke of bad luck if they had found us. We went up there when it was still light outside and came back down in the morning when it was light. And the nights were horrible! The Russians came every night! "Where are the women? Where are the women?" My mother and the farmer's wife were already old, and the Russians didn't do anything to them – to neither one of them. Oh, yes, the farmer's wife had Ruth and the boy, Kurt – the children. She had the two children down there, and the Russians didn't do anything to them. Of course, my mother and the farmer's wife dressed up like old women with head scarves and really looked horrible. And every evening and every night we had to hear the screaming down there. My God, how we trembled. I'll never forget it in my life. I was pregnant, and my mother was afraid that I would go into early labour. Karin was born in 1941, and the twins in 1945. They were so small. And then the Russians didn't come anymore. Oh, no, wait a minute. I forgot something.

There was a Russian officer there who spoke German well – a certain Vanya Volekoff. He settled in our house. He was a captain or had the rank of a captain – yes, yes, he was the one in charge. And he made sure that the roof of our house was repaired and that the doors and shutters were fixed so that they shut. He settled in there. And we were able to go home. We went into our house. It was good that we had him. Every night the Russian soldiers came back. Those were always the soldiers who were passing through in the direction of Berlin. It was always this route, but with different soldiers. The Russians marched through, but they wanted to have women during the night and that's why there was always rape in the village. It was horrible. Once we had the captain in our house, and whenever the Russian soldiers knocked on the door or vandalized the house, he immediately went outside. You can imagine how he shouted. I already mentioned to you that he really gave them the works. They were supposed to keep on passing through.

The Russian captain was in the village again after the war and wanted to see our family. This is what I heard from an acquaintance whom I visited. Our husbands had been at the ammunition depot back then – her husband and my husband. And we knew one another. And she told me that. She said: "Do you know who was here? He asked about you and about Karin and about mother and about father." And she told him that I had been in Recklinghausen in the west for a long time. My husband and I lived in Recklinghausen most of the time with my mother. My father died in the meantime in the east. He didn't live in our house, but rather in the farmer's house where we had been hiding in the hay in the barn. That's where my father died. He stayed over there and didn't come with us to the west.

Libusa Schibrowski was born in Berlin in 1919. She recalls some of the atrocities which happened during the Russian invasion of Berlin.

I got married to my husband in 1957, and he was a widower at that time. During the last days of the war – during the last days of April – his wife was shot dead by Russians because she refused to go along with them. They wanted to rape her or take her along, and she refused – she had her daughter along – and didn't want to go with them. They shot her in the stomach, and she bled to death in the courtyard. When my husband returned home from the prisoner-of-war camp, he never got over it when he discovered that his wife was dead. He never forgot it.

Did you witness things like this?

Not personally. But these things did happen. We had to leave our home and spend a whole week in a parish centre in Zehlendorf – I should say camp out on a mattress on the floor. Before all of this started, I received 10 pounds of margarine from a friend and carried it along with me in a small backpack – which was practically the only thing that saved our lives afterwards – and also the lives of others who used our margarine in the communal kitchen. What I want to say is that my father had a large rental property in Berlin – not where we were living – but in Schöneberg. It was a building on the corner of a street – pretty large – and my mother, my sister, and I went there after having spent an entire week in the parish centre. We thought that maybe we could stay there somewhere – or something like that. We used to have a cleaning woman there who had taken care of the building for years. She told us to go into one of the flats because a party member used to live there and had disappeared. He never came back anymore. She said: "Why don't you take it? Otherwise other people will." Back then, that's the way it was. Whichever building was empty, was then occupied. And we did it.

I was 25 years old at that time – but in this building there were two young girls – both of them were 15 or 16 years old. And both of them had been raped by the Russians, and they never forgot it their entire lives. Afterwards, they were somehow mentally disturbed. One was never able to be together with a man, and the other lived without a partner her whole life. That was the effect that it had. I felt so sorry for them. I knew the two girls from earlier because they were our tenants. And you couldn't do anything about it. And I also knew about an older woman who lived in the building. She later said: "For a loaf of bread I would do anything." That also existed. Before she starved – yes, those were other times. I always thought to myself: "Dear God, please don't let this happen to me." And there was actually no physical contact. It was a bad time in general.

Brandenburg

Ingrid Koppe was born in Berlin-Kreuzberg. Her father died on the Russian Front in 1941, and she was left alone with her mother and four sisters. She recalls the advance of Russian soldiers on Berlin in 1945 and events following the war.

At the beginning of 1945, the Russians came closer and closer. We wondered whether we should flee, but then we thought that it was useless. We were 50 kilometres away from Berlin: Where were we supposed to go? What were we supposed to do? The Russians were in our district by the end of March and the beginning of April. The administrative district city of Calau defended itself for four days – it had 4,000 inhabitants. It had a very strong Nazi district leader. He was of the opinion that the city had to be defended so that the assault on Berlin could be prevented.

We left the area of the factory. There were a lot of woods, and we knew the woods really well because we picked blueberries there as children. And we hid in the woods. We were in the woods for six days until the fighting was over in the administrative district city and then returned to our flat, but were immediately met by Russians. My mother was terribly afraid for my two older sisters who were then 13 and 14 years old. And she herself was also afraid although we were really a family unit. We later developed into a very strong unit without our father. That has actually remained until today. All five of us got married, and we are still a very strong family although my eldest sister has died in the meantime, and also two brothers-in-law; my husband's brothers, who married my sisters have passed away. And we believe that this resulted from the events and experiences of the war.

In 1945 we experienced the Russians at first hand, whereby I have to say that the first wave of troops was horrible. We were really afraid. They stood in front of us with machine guns and wanted to have women. There were five families who had all come from Berlin. We all joined together and made large night camps. The children slept there, and the women hid under the beds. We said that there were only children. The Russians behaved well there. They didn't do anything to children I have to add. After the first wave of Russians passed through – which included a large number of Mongolians I have to say – I saw the first Mongolians in my life – the next wave brought along very good, civilized, and well-behaved Russians. They also gave us bread and food because there basically wasn't anything in this early period. You had to see how you got along. A horse was shot, and everyone ran there and slaughtered it. They kept the meat cool, and then we lived on horse meat for a few days. These are the things that we experienced. The farmers brought us a few potatoes because they were able to feed themselves, but we basically didn't have anything. We sometimes waited four or five hours for bread, and then we received about half a loaf for six people. It was really difficult. There were a lot of people who had been evacuated from the area around Berlin. And, after the surrender of Germany, the Russians said that if we were from Berlin then we should return to Berlin.

The surrender was on 8 May, and we returned to Berlin on foot. All five families joined together and formed a group. I can still remember that my mother took along my youngest sister who was four years old. She pushed the baby stroller, and we pulled a cart behind us. We returned to Berlin and slept in barns. We saw rats running around at night. Then we went through the woods in Calau near Berlin – it is also a small town. Calau defended itself so fiercely. We passed through the woods there, and it stunk horribly. My mother said: "Don't look! Don't look!" There were still arms and legs of soldiers everywhere. They hadn't been cleared away. There were helmets with the heads still inside. It was really horrible when we walked through these woods. But we arrived in Berlin and were taken into a so-called "reception camp". They first assigned us a basement flat with one and a half rooms. We lived there and went through the cold season in 1945–46.

After everything had calmed down, we had a police curfew in Berlin. Everyone had to be off the streets by 11:00 pm. We ended up in the American sector of Berlin. And then my mother said: "There are train connections again." That was in September 1945. It was possible to travel down to Lusatia. We went to the train station in Schöneweide. And then they said that there was a train that went down to the Spree

Forest. And we had to change trains with the little pushcart from track to track. The train left at night and didn't stop until Senftenberg. And after my mother saw that we were already in Senftenberg, which was past Calau, she said: "Get out! Out! Out!" because we were afraid that we would land in the Russian zone without knowing where we were. And then we got out in Senftenberg and walked back to Calau. There we got a few things back that we had left in a room after we had been bombed out. My elder sister and I loaded the items onto the cart. My eldest sister remained with the youngest ones in Berlin. We wanted to return by train, but there weren't any trains anymore. And then we walked about 40 kilometres from this house to Berlin. There were trucks that stopped on the motorway and wanted to take us along. We had heard from others that as soon as the luggage was loaded on top of vehicles that they drove off and people would stand there without luggage. And we didn't want that to happen so we kept on walking.

And then we came to the city limits of Berlin, and there was a Russian checkpoint. And we basically didn't have any permission to enter the Russian zone again and to pick things up. The Russian commander – or whoever it was – came to us and said: "Do you have a permit?" My mother said: "No." [He said:] "Then you're not allowed to take these things along with you. And if you don't have it, then we first have to check the things at the post headquarters." And, of course, we were really afraid. My mother said to us: "A truck is coming back there. Once they open up the gate and check it, the two of you should pull the cart, and I'll push it. And then we'll walk through." We did it, and the two of us in front were running. We were afraid that they would shoot, and mother was pushing from behind. But they didn't do anything at all. They must have been so perplexed that they let us keep running – maybe because we were almost children. At that time, I was 11 and my sister 13 years old. We were very small and basically undernourished. For adults, we were still children at that age. And then we walked to Berlin. It was horrible. We had walked 40 kilometres in two days with a push-cart at the ages of 11 and 13. We arrived home at five minutes before eleven and were able to drive the cart through the gate. And my eldest sister was really afraid: She was 14 years old and home alone with the two smallest children who were 4 and 9 years old. And they were happy that we were there again.

Bavaria

Anna Kreise was born in the Ore Mountains in 1930. She recalls the Russian occupation of Germany in 1945.

The schools were all bombed and destroyed. And, as diligent as I was, I helped out in a military hospital as a high school student. After I had been there for only a short time, they said that the Russians were coming. I was 15 years old, and the Front was coming closer. And they decided – I don't know who decided it because it came from the top – that Prague should become a military hospital city. That's what they were talking about at that time. They arranged for a large train to be used for all the injured soldiers. And they said to me: "Come along, it will be horrible if you remain here because the Russians are coming." And, of course, they needed nurses because they had very few. I went along and helped the severely injured by giving them something to eat and to drink and to do whatever I could. We never reached Prague. Shortly before Prague the train stopped; the Russians were waiting there, and took everyone off the train who could walk. I was so clever that I noticed how two slightly injured soldiers went off on their own. I went with them and disappeared. We wanted to make our way through a forest near my hometown in the Ore Mountains. As I child we often used to go skiing there, and I knew my way around. I said to them: "If we make it that far, then we can go to our skiing lodge and hide there." But we didn't make it that far. When we crossed a road, the Americans were suddenly standing there. They took us along and brought us to a large field. There were hundreds of soldiers there: everyone possible – nurses and soldiers. And then the enlisted men walked around the whole time with billy clubs and made sure there was order and that no one left. We didn't get anything at all to eat for at least three days. Nothing at all. Neither to drink nor to eat. And the worst part was that we were all a bit ill. We tried to use the dandelions in the fields for a soup. We were more or less ill and got diarrhoea.

On the fourth day, the Russians returned. And, I have to say, that saved me. They divided us up and took away the injured soldiers. And there weren't so many injured soldiers anymore. The ones who weren't so injured remained in the freight cars, but I don't know what happened to the others. In any case, they transported us to Czechoslovakia again, which wasn't far away. Oberwiesenthal isn't far from the Czech border. They brought us to a large school together with injured soldiers and took care of us as well as they could. They didn't have anything themselves or very little. In retrospect, I have to say that those were very decent people. They tried to help us, but how were they supposed to help without medication? They brought us everything that was available from that area such as concentrated butter – but what could you do with concentrated butter if you didn't have any bread to put it on? They at least tried to keep us alive. I can't tell you how long that went on – but I believe it lasted for fourteen days. And then suddenly they said: "You're all going to Russia to a prisoner-of-war camp." I wasn't really shocked because they were very friendly to us. There was a doctor there – a Jew – I still remember him today. And I would say that they were decent to us. I can't actually say whether they were only nice to me because I was a young girl.

From there I came to a town called Sorau-Sagan which is now in Poland. We were taken off the train and came to another camp which consisted of evacuated buildings. It was an entire street that had been blocked off, and we lived there more or less. It was rather far away, but we couldn't leave. Where were we supposed to go? And then there was again the problem about who would take care of the ill soldiers – among them were severely injured Russian soldiers. Very few people were willing to sign up for the work, but I thought: "Go ahead and sign up." I reported to them and took care of the severely injured Russian soldiers the entire time, some of whom had typhoid fever or spotted fever. That must have impressed them so much – I really did it from the bottom of my heart – some were very young soldiers who were 20 years old. The Russians had an entirely different manner than the English or the Americans. First, they were always homesick and talked about home. The word "домой" is still in my ears today. They all wanted to go "home" to their families. What I especially noticed was that we did a lot of bad things in Russia – we can't ignore that – I met a lot of young

Russians whose parents or brothers and sisters had been killed – but what I never experienced, and that's what I always told my husband, is that they weren't hateful. You know? I never experienced the emotion of hatred in them. On the contrary, they also felt pity for us. It was very touching: When they had something to eat, they often shared it and gave us half. I experienced that as great human actions back then. They were the victors, weren't they?

Your story is unusual.

No, it isn't.

Most people tell stories about the brutality of the Russians and that the women had to hide.

That was only in the beginning. Those were the troops on the Front. When they came into our cities and saw the nicely dressed girls, and those were all really young men, they raped them. I have to say the following: that certainly happened – not only once – but many times. However, those were predominantly the troops on the Front. But when you worked together with the Russians, which I had to do as a matter of course, you experienced a great deal of humanity over and over again. I was released early, covered with lice, because they recognized that I worked so hard. They said: "You can go home. You were always a good worker." They acknowledged that. I returned home shortly before Christmas 1945.

Lower Saxony

Christine Kahl recalls the occupation of Neuhaus an der Elbe (Lower Saxony) by Russian soldiers.

Neuhaus an der Elbe was a prohibited area for a long time because it was 6 kilometres behind the border. The Russian military command was there, and they were very strict. The Russian soldiers were not allowed to bother Germans. I can make that claim. And my father-in-law, an elderly gentleman, played cards with them. You were able to look into the windows of the small houses there, and Russian soldiers would knock on the glass. He played cards with them. They tossed their money onto the table and played cards together. And if they ever said: "You, girl … come along," my father-in-law would say: "None of that." And they were very peaceful. And they were very friendly to children. One person in our group always went to pick up milk. She told the Russians that she had a baby and that's why she needed the milk. Afterwards, she was afraid to go onto the streets because the Russians really wanted to see the baby. I have to say that I never experienced anything horrible with the Russians. Maybe that was because if you said to them the words "Russian military command", they were gone immediately. It was very strict for them. The horrible things that happened with the first wave of Russians, never happened anymore. But, as I said, I had my husband, who was my friend, at my side, who took care of me anyway.

Harz Mountains

Amalie Schlebusch was born in Bonn in 1929. She remembers an incident in Stapelburg (Harz Mountains) while travelling west with her four younger brothers and sisters during Russian occupation in 1945.

We were at the train station, and the Russians came inside and asked: "Who has a musical instrument?" A young man said: "I do." The Russian asked him: "Where?" The young man said: "At home. A piano." And they took him outside and beat him to death. We all heard him screaming. They didn't tolerate any joking.

CHAPTER V

THE WESTERN ADVANCE

American Drive into Belgium (September 1944)

Wilhelmine Schiffer was born in Geilenkirchen in 1924. At the age of 19, she worked as a secretary for the company Junker in Liège, Belgium, which produced tracks for tanks. She recalls the advance of the American Army from the west and the evacuation of the company headquarters in 1944.

I remember exactly when the Americans came in September 1944. I didn't leave Liège by train – normally it was by train, but the train connections had been interrupted. I crossed the border in some car in order to get home. And then they said that the company Junker was to be evacuated to Gevelsberg. They knew that the Americans were coming. And during this night – I believe that the Americans entered Lammersdorf on 12 September or the beginning of September – our company was supposed to be evacuated and a meeting point near Lammersdorf had been arranged. But during the night I was supposed to work on the teleprinter. And my family in Monschau – my mother and my sister – also had to be evacuated. I was supposed to work the night shift for the company in Gevelsberg and then go to my mother.

I had a very old bicycle and didn't have a car. And there were no train connections anymore. And half way to where I had to go, I got a flat tyre in Monschau. And I couldn't keep on riding. Soldiers streamed past me, and I was wedged in between trucks and so on. I arrived late in Lammersdorf, and when I got to the company there weren't any lights on. There wasn't any electricity, so working on the teleprinter was useless. And Lammersdorf was under fire. In front of our company there were one-man bunkers – protective bunkers for just one person. And I remember in the morning running from one bunker to the next in order to get to my boss's house. I was supposed to go to him because the technical director, the sales director, and another director remained behind. And I was supposed to leave with these three directors on the following morning. I went to this family. I was 20 years old. And my boss had to take care of me.

And then the Americans came. I remember how afraid we were when we saw the first American soldiers coming with their rifles aimed. I don't remember how many people remained behind. Lammersdorf was occupied by the Americans from September [1944] until spring 1945. It was the first line of the Front. Simmerath was always German and was first captured in the spring. Simmerath was 5 or 7 kilometres away. We were on the first line of the Front. And we couldn't be moved back by the Americans because the other villages had been occupied. We had a curfew. The men remaining behind had to milk the cows twice a day which the Americans herded together in a large area. The men had to go out in the morning to milk the cows and take care of the animals. And we didn't have any electricity anymore. The waterlines didn't work anymore, and we went to wells to get the water. So, we were busy getting what we needed during the two hours we were allowed out in the mornings and the evenings.

I lived together with my boss and his family: His wife was still there, his mother was still there, and his two children were still there. We couldn't go any further and stayed there. We got food and potatoes from the empty houses which had been evacuated by the Americans and made it through the entire winter somehow. We were on the first line of the Front. And, I believe, the Americans replaced their soldiers or staff every fourteen days. We quickly went into the houses where they had been and took the packages of rations. That was the first time that I had ever seen American paperback books in horizontal format. Do you know them? I took them and read them.

Military Field Hospitals (February 1945)

Doris Pfannschmidt was born in 1917 in Lobositz in Sudetenland (Czechoslovakia). She worked as a nurse in a military hospital in Dijon, Reims, Bordeaux, and Lourdes in France. She describes her work at a military field hospital near Landstuhl (Rhineland-Palatinate) during an eight-week military offensive against the Allied forces at the beginning of 1945.

For the most part, our day began with the work schedule for the surgeons. We had four surgeons. Some of them wanted to perform the large operations, which they called "stomach matters", meaning that they had to be worked on immediately – and couldn't wait – and took four hours. They preferred to do these things more than a lot of small operations with shrapnel from shells. They worked simultaneously in four operating rooms. And during this time, the medical secretary – which was my job at that time – was also responsible for sterilizing the instruments and doing similar things which had to be done on the side. And I had to write it all down along with the results.

The doctors found it very difficult to decide when soldiers could be transported again. This was because the military hospital was full of patients who were lined up in the hallways with serious injuries such as burns from plane crashes. These were really horrible things so that the patients weren't able to be transported at all. This was the situation for the most part. Often, they died beforehand. But all of this had to be recorded for administrative purposes. This was decided during the rounds. And the decisions made in the operating rooms and during the rounds were passed on to the medical orderlies – mostly non-commissioned officers – who asked for a certain number of medical transporters with space to sit down or lie down. It eased the burden on the doctors because they knew that they could fill these beds again. This is the way it was the entire day without a lunch break. There also weren't many breaks during the night.

We had good rations. We received a lot of coffee and cigarettes – which we all smoked. Today we would have second thoughts. But back then we certainly needed it, and that's the reason we did it. That's the way it was the entire day and at least half of the night. They scheduled us for three or four hours of sleep. And if it was possible – and there weren't any air raids – we took advantage of the opportunity and went to sleep for a few hours. And the next day we got up at seven and started it all over again.

What kind of psychological burden was it for you?

Well, today you can't imagine it. It was important work that we did because people were helped and everything continued to move along so that patients were released, although injured soldiers continued to arrive. Of course, you couldn't think about the reason for these injuries – it was certainly idiotic that they had done all these things. But if no one had been there, then it certainly would have been much worse.

American Occupation (1945)

Married couple in Nickenich on the Rhine wish to remain anonymous. The husband remained at home during the war because he was unfit for military service. They recall American troops occupying their village in May 1945.

Husband: The Americans came with a few tanks and one of them was parked on the corner here right next to my parents' house. And by chance, I was there because I lived nearby. They were parked there with their gun barrels pointed in the direction of Andernach. As bold as I was, I went out and stood on the edge of the street and watched them. Suddenly I noticed how they aimed their guns in the direction of Andernach. And I didn't think it would happen. Boom! They fired. I thought that my ears would fly off. [laughs] The windows on the left side [of the street] were all gone. They were all broken. I thought: "You stupid guys can't frighten me. I'm staying here." And I remained standing.

Wife: When the Americans were outside, there were some men who came and wanted to fire a bazooka.

Husband: At that moment, my father and some disbanded German soldiers were standing there. One of them had a bazooka and wanted to fire it. My father and a neighbour said: "Stop! Stop! Put that thing away! They'll come here with their planes and bomb everything." They listened to reason and took the bazooka and stood it up against the wall in the courtyard. It was there for three weeks until the heavy garbage was picked up.

Wife: The Americans were gone for a few days and then came back again. My parents were visiting us, and within half an hour we had to pick up and leave. We were only able to take along necessities. I had our clothing in a basket in the basement, and we loaded it onto a cart. Necessities. We only took along bed linen and things like that. And then we strolled through the village with our horse-drawn cart. My mother lived on the street behind the church. That's where we went with all our things. Seventeen of us were living there.

Husband: People were sleeping everywhere.

Wife: When I went to our house, I was shocked because Americans were sleeping in my bed with their dirty boots.

Husband: They wanted to secure the entrance to the village so that no-one could come in or out. That was in the direction of the Rhine. It was a strategic point.

Wife: But you were allowed go into the house every day – only at certain times. And they were really nice guys.

Husband: Especially when they saw our women. [laughs]

Wife: I'm not kidding you when I tell you that we had such a large can of cooking lard in my kitchen cupboard. And in the oven of the coal-burning stove we had small cans with flour and cheese spread and coffee. We also had it in small cans. My godmother really liked to drink coffee.

Husband: Those were our emergency rations.

Wife: I didn't like coffee back then.

Husband: Soldiers always like to see beautiful women or women in general. No matter whether they are German women or not. It doesn't matter.

Wife: Those were nice guys who didn't bother us. You were always there. One time Till was along. She was 16 years old. That is my youngest sister. She was 16. She was along, and a soldier came and wrapped his arm around her. She resisted, and he turned red. And he never tried it again. [laughs] So you can't say bad things about them.

Husband: They took certain things from the house.

Wife: I had such nice embroidered things. A tablecloth and things on the wall.

Husband: Souvenirs.

Wife: They took them along.

Husband: They took a few of my watches from the closet. We couldn't take everything with us. It happened so fast.

Wife: We couldn't load everything onto the cart in half an hour. Oh yes, I went downstairs and one of them said that I should take the mattresses outside. We only had to cross the street. There is a path through the fields which leads to my mother's backyard.

Husband: We took the mattresses along with us rather than leaving them where they were. They took one of our tables. A nice big table. They thought: "How can we use a table?" The soldiers took it along. [laughs] Soldiers take what they want. We probably did it, too.

Wife: And they stole another old table. A teacher lived upstairs in the house. And she wasn't here at that time.

Husband: The teacher wasn't here and had wine in the cellar. They went and got the wine and drank it.

Wife: It would have gone bad because she didn't drink anyway. [laughs] It would have gone bad. [laughs]

Husband: Otherwise, we can't complain about the things that happened in this village.

Elisabeth Hartmann was born in Henrichenburg in North Rhine-Westphalia in 1920. She was working as a hotel cook in Wiehl during the war and recalls American soldiers first occupying the town in 1945.

What happened at the end of the war?

We suddenly noticed that the German soldiers were retreating. They were extremely tired and worn down and wounded and sick and one of them was on a motor bike. That's how they started the retreat. And the next day, we were supposed to pick up groceries somewhere. And that's how we got caught in the Front. We saw German soldiers standing behind every house with bazookas, and then we got caught in the Front. German soldiers were moving in the direction of Gummersbach.

What did you see in town?

Nobody was there. It was deadly silent. Until two Americans snuck up in front of us – they weren't far away and shouted: "Hands up!" And then we fled and ran into the town hall. The door to the town hall was open, but nobody was there. And then we went into the basement, and there were a lot of employees – and they were all in the basement. And then we said: "The Americans are coming! The Americans are coming!" The mayor and his staff went upstairs and negotiated with the Americans. He surrendered or raised the white flag. And then someone said that the town hall was burning. We had to get out. And then we went home on a secret path over barbed wire. When we arrived at home, we also saw soldiers standing there – Americans. And when we went into the house through the basement, one of the girls shouted out: "Heil Hitler! We're back again."

The wife of the local party leader hid her picture of Hitler – with a wonderful frame – in my bed. And then the Americans asked us whether we were Nazis. One after the other everyone said: "No Nazi. No Nazi." And I thought that it was really stupid. I said: "Yes, Nazi." And then I had to stand up against the wall, and one of the soldiers shot at me – and just missed me.

Why did he do that? And why did you say that you were a Nazi?

Just because. He did it because he found the picture of Adolf Hitler in my bed. The other woman hid it there because she wanted to save it.

Hubert Stellmach was born in Oppeln in Upper Silesia in 1932. He fled from Russian forces in January 1945 and travelled by train via Breslau to Bavaria. He describes the American occupation in Bavaria.

It was exactly on 12 April 1945 – I remember it because it was my father's birthday – that the Americans marched into the district of Kulmbach [in Bavaria] and occupied it. We were able to continue living there. Since my father wasn't there and our savings accounts had been frozen, we lived from social welfare because there wasn't any money.

How were the American soldiers?

It depended on the soldiers. At that time, we were living at a ranger's lodge. There were some Americans who were very rough. I remember a story about the ranger's son who was also a soldier: The Americans broke into his desk and found a pistol. They made him undress, stood him against the wall, and wanted to shoot him. But they didn't do it. I have to mention one thing: The politest and nicest soldiers were the Blacks. I remember the following incident: We were standing in a room – the other soldiers didn't care – but the Black soldier asked whether he was allowed to smoke. Since there was no ashtray, he tapped the ash onto his hand and carried it outside. [laughs] The other soldiers searched all the rooms and took whatever they wanted. They especially liked wristwatches. The Protestant military bishop later jokingly remarked that the USA stood for "Uhrensammlerarmee" [Watch Collectors Army]. [laughs] There was a great difference in how they behaved.

Did you experience any bad things?

I saw that a German soldier – who was far away – ran across the lawn in a park and was shot down by an American soldier with a machine gun although he wasn't a threat in any way. [weeps]

CHAPTER VI

AFTERMATH OF THE WAR

Expulsion from Sudetenland

Elisabeth Bost was born in 1924 in Chomutov in the Sudetenland. Her German ancestors settled in this area in the eleventh century. She recalls the annexation of Czechoslovakia by the Nazis in 1938 and the expulsion of the German population by the Czechs in 1945.

What happened at the end of the war?

The Russians marched into Chomutov. The quarter that we lived in was completely blocked off. The commanding general and his staff settled into the houses. Across the way was a free piece of land where the Russians kept their horses. And we had Russians quartered in our home. There was a colonel or a lieutenant – I don't remember exactly. And we girls hid in the attic. He made a good impression and brought some friends along. They celebrated in those rooms. And he saw me and was really annoyed that I was hiding from him. He said that I didn't have to do that. Well, alright. And one day the Russians marched off. And the Czechs came.

The so-called "Národní Výbor" [National Committee] was established. The administration of the city was carried out by the Czechs. And the Germans all had to wear white armbands in order to be recognized as such. And, at the beginning of June – I believe – the streets were closed, and all the men between the ages of 12 and 65 had to go the sport grounds – to the so-called "Jahn Sport Grounds" and assemble there. They separated the men who were in the SS. There was the so-called "Homeland SS". They didn't harm anyone – such as the director of Mannesman, and a senior high school teacher from the teacher training centre, and a gym teacher, and so on. And these German Prisoners were terribly mistreated. They carved swastikas into their backs. I don't know how many people were involved – there were also people there who were injured in the war. The border to Germany was only 20 or 30 kilometres away. You had to travel through the mountains: there were the Bohemian Ore Mountains on this side and the Saxon Ore Mountains on the other side. And they wanted to hand over these German men and children to the Russians, but the Russians refused. They said: "What are we going to do with these men? Our country is so poor. How are we supposed to transport them?" There were some old men and children and soldiers injured in the war. And then they forced these men down to Maltheuern – to the hydrogenation plant that was covered with bomb craters.[1] They had to do the clean-up work there. And many of them met their death: They were shot by the Czechs for the smallest triviality. I have just read a book by a fellow schoolmate who experienced this. Those were terrible conditions. As I said, that was the male population of Chomutuv.

We experienced one of the first evacuations on 21 June [1945]. Our entire quarter was blocked off. And my grandfather died on that same morning. He was 87 years old and had fallen. The post office senior officer in Chomutov lived on the first floor flat of our building. And he said: "Give me your jewellery. Give me your silverware. And I'll help you." He did this. He showed people grandfather's dead body. And he said: "Don't you have any respect for the dead?" And they gave us a reprieve until August so that we had the chance to prepare somewhat – to be expelled. They only gave you fifteen to twenty minute's time in order to pack things together – and no one was ready to leave permanently. It was an advantage that I worked in the pharmacy.

And, as I said, the next evacuation came in August. We first came to a hutted camp – we had to leave our building of flats. And a Czech came to stay in the flat where I lived together with my mother and my grandmother. He took over the flat. We came to a camp. I managed to get two small baby carriages – I had a few down blankets and something to eat. Most importantly, my mother had our documents, my father's will, and so on. She took all those things along. Actually, you weren't allowed to, but they couldn't check everything. We were in this camp for eight days, and then we were brought to the border by freight train – not in a passenger train. And we were let out of the freight car. My mother and my grandmother remained in the courtyard of an inn. They put down some straw on the ground. The young people had to leave the entire area, and we went to Leipzig on foot. From there we went to Torgau. And from there we continued to Frankfurt [on the Oder]. The journey was horrible – we slept under the stars, even with the small children who were along.

And then we heard about a place to stay in Muldenstein. And from there we went in the direction of Bitterfeld. There were subsistence homesteads, many of which were built during the Nazi period. And we were supposed to move into the barracks that were deserted by the Russians – it was impossible. They were full of bugs and lice and had to first be cleaned. And we were assigned to individual buildings. I brought my mother and my grandmother there under difficult circumstances. There were very nice, helpful people there. They rebuilt their houses themselves, gutted them out, and so on. And they said that we should help other people in return when the war was over and we had all our possessions.

Forced from Silesia

Herbert Schink was born in Schönbrunn in the district of Leobschütz in Upper Silesia in 1932. He remembers his flight from advancing Russian troops in March 1945, his return to Upper Silesia after the surrender of Germany in May 1945, and expulsion by the Poles in June 1946.

In 1945, the Front came closer and closer. The Russians entered Upper Silesia and came into our district, and we had to leave while they were being held up. There was an incredible amount of military mobilization and so on. On 16 March 1945 we were forced to flee. The reason was that a large military movement was expected – the entire population had to leave. We left by horse and wagon. At 9:00 pm low-flying planes were underway, and the Russians were about 10 kilometres away from our village. We could hear the multiple rocket launchers and see the mobilization and the shooting and fire in the distance. At 9:00 pm we had to leave the village of Schönbrunn and travel across the Sudetenland by horse and wagon until shortly before Prague. But we never reached the Americans who met the Russians there.

And then we were forced to travel back again. That was in May [1945]. The war was already over. That's how long we were on the road with horse and wagon. More or less. We were able to spend nights along the way with farmers in their barns. On our way home, the Russians came towards us in the euphoria of victory. They took the horses away from us, our wagons remained standing on the road, and people were forced to make their way with only the clothes on their backs. The women ran naked into the cornfields and spent the night there to escape from being raped. We arrived in our village again at the end of May 1945, but weren't allowed to enter because of the large Russian military hospital now located at the school. A mass grave with 360 Russian soldiers was in the schoolyard. It was unbelievable what had happened during the war. Dead German soldiers were scattered in ditches along the road and in the fields – swarms of flies landed on them. Some of these soldiers were buried and others were not. It was horrible.

Then the Poles came in June 1945. Some of them in the east had also been resettled by the Russians and were now supposed to live in Upper Silesia. We were supposed to be evacuated. From 1945–46, the Poles took over our farms as they wished and settled down. They were the new owners. When we fled on 16 March [1945], we left everything standing just the way it was. And when we came back, nothing was there – no animals, nothing – windows were broken, the beds defecated, and everything destroyed. All hell had broken loose. As I said, the Poles came in 1945, and we lived together with them on our farms in 1946. In that year, people died of typhoid fever. We didn't have anything to eat. We put wheat into the meat grinder just to get something into our stomachs. In June 1946, we were told that all Germans had to wait on the street with hand luggage. We were forced to leave like cattle and go to the district capital – the Poles carried Kalashnikovs. They searched us and took away everything that we had recovered or saved after returning from our flight. And then we were forced to leave in cattle cars to Leobschütz. The Poles drove us out like cattle – as I said. There were thirty-five of us in each cattle car. They threw a metal bucket inside as a toilet. We didn't know if we were being sent to Russia.

We were transported to the west and were on the train the entire time. The first stop on the train was in Warendorf [in North Rhine-Westphalia]. It was there that we were able to stay in horse stables on straw and received medical attention and got something to eat. Then we continued to Lette near Coesfeld where we stayed in war barracks and received medical treatment. Of course, refugees needed a place to stay. We were distributed among the villages in Darfeld, Osterwick, Lette, and as far south as Bocholt. We stood on the market square, and the farmers came and chose people who were able to work. We found a place in Holtwick in Westphalia with farmers. Our family was divided into three parts: My parents went to a farmer, and my brother and I went to another farmer – I was still a school boy and had to go to school – and my sister to another family. We lived with farmers, scattered apart from one another from

1946 when we were expelled until 1953, so that we could earn money to eat. Then we got a flat here in Coesfeld, and the family was brought together again shortly before Christmas. I'll never forget it – there were six of us – we received a small flat – thank God that we finally managed to do so. My father was disabled with a bad hip because of the military campaign in Poland and couldn't work in Westphalia. The flat had three rooms for six people. I'll never forget it – it was shortly before Christmas and the family was together again for the first time. We wiped away each other's tears.

Driven from Pomerania

Gerda Reiser was born in 1927 in Liebenow in Pomerania. After fleeing from advancing Russian troops, she returned to her home in Pomerania and was then driven out by Polish settlers.

Shortly after the war, we returned home from up north near Stralsund. Even our cat was still there. That was in May [1945]. And in June – around the twentieth – we had to leave Liebenow in the district of Greifenhagen in the governmental district of Stettin. We were there for four weeks at the most, but I can't tell you exactly how long. And they told us that the land belonged to Poland, and we had to leave. We wanted to take along as many things as possible, which we couldn't because we weren't able to carry everything. It was a hot summer. We only took along the most important things which were readily available such as something to wear or something to eat. It was a hot summer. We hardly took anything along. It was impossible to carry things. There were a lot of us because our village had approximately 1,000 inhabitants, but many died while they were fleeing the first time. There were many who had died along the road – people and horses were left in ditches under fruit trees. It was winter. It was February. It was a cold winter. That was from Liebenow to near Stralsund. The name of the place was Fuhlendorf in the district of Franzburg-Barth.

First, we had to go north until the war was over, and then we were allowed to return home. And after four weeks we had to leave again. It was very difficult to go, and then to be at home shortly, and then to leave for good. We had to leave a lot of things behind. It was really horrible. It was really horrible. We weren't rich and didn't have our own things. We had to learn how to work for different land owners with mills and didn't earn much money. Every year we were able to slaughter one pig. And we had a goat in our stable and a small vegetable garden. And we did alright.

Stealing Coal to Survive

Aneliese Emmel was born in Cologne in 1913. She spent the war years in Bonn while her husband was away at war in France. In the final year of the war, rations were extremely low for her and her two children.

What did you do while your husband was away at war?

I stole coal so that I had something to heat with. We were at the train station. You know? And then we went into the fields and gathered the remains of the harvested potatoes that were still in the ground. And then they caught us, and I had to go to the police. That was the last year of the war. When my husband came home from the war, he took care of the matter at the police station on the Rhine. They caught us, you know? [she laughs] And luckily my husband returned from the prisoner-of-war camp. That's where he was before that. And they noticed us, but we didn't do anything else. We were just digging up the potatoes from the ground.

You were just digging up potatoes?

Yes, the remains. You know, the parts that were still in the ground. The fields had been cleared. They had already harvested the potatoes. And then we stole the coal at the train station. When the trains came in, we quickly took some and put them in our sacks and went back home. We were lucky. And then they caught us. It was a difficult time.

Disciplinary Action

Christine Kahl was born in Bonn in 1924. She was working as a nurse in Cologne in 1945 when she asked Nazi officers for food for ten orphan children. Three days later, she received her draft notice ordering her to report for duty at a military airfield to service night bombers.

I wanted to get food for ten children. And they told me to go to a farm with the children. I answered: "You're sitting here, filling your bellies, gorging yourselves and boozing." They answered: "What are you getting excited about? Don't worry, just go home." And three days later I had to go for my medical examination for military service. From there, I was transported by truck to Verl to a military airfield to service night bombers. Every morning, I had to clean the planes. That was in February 1945. I had a pay book which I threw away when the Americans arrived.

I felt that this was punishment because I had insulted those officers. My father said to me: "Child, I cannot protect you. You have to go along." I went for my medical examination, received a uniform as an anti-aircraft helper, and, as I said, went to work at a military airfield. Every morning when the planes landed – we had only three planes – they had to be serviced, the ammunition unloaded, everything dried and loaded back onto the planes, and prepared for take-off in the evenings. I celebrated my [twenty-first] birthday there. And then the first Americans crossed the Rhine. We left Verl through the Teutoburg Forest as far as Völkenrode, again to a military airfield. There wasn't anyone there anymore, so we were left on our own. But we had papers for northern Germany. We were supposed to report at every checkpoint. I wanted to try to escape, but it wasn't possible because they forced us through towns while carrying rifles. We were brought to the next train, again to the next military command, and so on. We were moving in the direction of the north so that the new "Fourth Reich" could be established. Unfortunately, they continued onto the other side of the Elbe

River – I couldn't swim – I didn't have any other possibility – some of them escaped – they swam across the Elbe and were gone.

After the Americans let us go, I ended up in Neuhaus an der Elbe and came to a family. It was very primitive there. I married the son of the family in order to get out of this misery. There were only refugees there. For me personally, it was really the bottom of the barrel: farmlands, outhouses, washing at the water pump, and so on. I wanted only to get out of there. The son loved me, and I said: "If you love me, you have to take me to the Rhineland. I won't stay here." He came along, and our marriage lasted forty-six years.

Diphtheria

Karla Geinert contracted toxic diphtheria at the age of 21 from her husband who returned home from the war. She describes her ailments and the one-year healing process.

The war was over and soon afterwards my hard life began. I got toxic diphtheria. My husband brought it along with him. I'm mentioning this extra because it's a severe form of normal diphtheria. You're blind for eight days, then your soft palate is paralysed, then you can't swallow anymore and all the fluids come out of your nose, then your neck is bigger than your head, and then you learn how to walk again on your knees because everything is paralysed. And if you were in a Catholic hospital in one room as a young married couple, then they had already hung up the cross outside the door and you had no chance. There wasn't any penicillin. Right? All of that didn't exist yet in 1945.

I believe the reason why we survived it so well was that children earlier were given cod liver oil for their strength from October to February. You're looking at me strangely. You've never had it? It tasted awful, but we didn't have any colds. We had the usual childhood diseases. But sniffles and coughing and pneumonia and things like that we didn't have although there was a biting wind and the winter was cold. The Rhine froze over twice during this time. If I tell doctors about this today during my examination, they look at me curiously because they know this made people rather strong back then. If my husband hadn't been a doctor, I would never have believed it. He remained calm. Maybe he was happy that he didn't have to look at me during the first eight days. [laughs] He always said: "Calm down, it will go away, there might be a few side effects. But it's possible to survive it." We believed in cod liver oil. However, we were more than handicapped for an entire year. But we were near our home and could eat butter and cream, while others were worse off. In reality, we had everything we needed. Those were the advantages of my upbringing on a farm.

Forced Repatriation to Russia

Oskar Neumann was born in Altkrausendorf (Stara Krasnica) in Ukraine in 1931. As an ethnic German, he was relocated from Ukraine to Germany in October 1943 along with retreating German soldiers and resettled in Silesia. After the war, he was repatriated by Russian occupying troops in eastern Germany near Leipzig and transported by freight train to a small village in the Ural Mountains in Russia, where he was subjected to forced labour. His release, along with that of thousands of other prisoners, was negotiated by German Federal Chancellor Adenauer in 1956, and he was granted permission to emigrate to Germany.

The Russians were coming closer. It was well understood that as an ethnic German, you had to serve with the Germans in the Wehrmacht. Everyone had to serve. If you hadn't yet served and were Ukrainian, you were taken along. Those of German descent had to leave with the Germans. We had to go along. It was October 1943. We weren't allowed to use the main roads through Poland as civilians. We travelled by horse and carriage. The whole family climbed on top and set off. Almost every family had a carriage, and we placed our suitcases on top. We brought clothing, bedding, and what little food we had. And we took the cows along with us. The German Wehrmacht told us that Ukrainians could stay, but those of German descent who had gone into hiding would be shot on the spot. They announced this on the radio and everywhere else. If a German didn't want to go along, they were shot right then and there. What were people supposed to do? They loaded the children and everything onto the wagons and set off. In October, we didn't go very far. We were in a large forest. We had to keep going. The Ukrainians would have killed us anyway. We could have either gone along or they would have slaughtered us.

We continued through this vast forest, and there were so many partisans. During the day, the German planes watched over us. We travelled as far as Shepetivka and the German Front stopped there. We also stopped there. We celebrated Christmas and New Year there and stayed until around March 1944. We were taken to Ukrainian villages, and every family had to accommodate us. The Germans arranged it, and the Ukrainians had to take us in.

How did the families react?

They were angry, but couldn't do anything about it. The Germans would have ... you know. We were in a village and stayed in the house of the mayor. He had two elder sons. There were ten of us, and we lived in a big room. There was a Russian stove where we slept. It was warmest upstairs where they slept. And there was a small kitchen. We lay on the floor, and the whole family slept there. They slept upstairs. The mother of the family cooked food with our mother. And they distilled schnapps together from sugar beets. [laughs loudly] They understood that we had no other choice. Our children were with theirs, and the partisans left us alone. My brother was 16 years old, and they had children who were 17 and 19 years old. They did everything together while we were there. Then we had to move on.

Did your family initially want to leave with the Germans?

No one wanted to leave their houses and vegetable gardens where they had always lived. But it was the only thing left for people. We had planted potatoes and had our cows. No one wanted to leave. And in the winter, we travelled through Galicia. We had to go on to Germany. We travelled for half a month and made a stop in Poland. There, we went to another village and lived with the Poles. I'm not sure whether it was Poland or Belarus. Some of them spoke Ukrainian. After a week, we took the train. The train station wasn't very far. They informed us all that we had to leave, and we had to go to the station and spent the night there. Many of the elderly slept in the carriages. It was snowing. Then the freight train arrived. They loaded all the horses and cows, and we went into another train car. And then we arrived in (phon.) Raditz in Silesia near Breslau. That was in Germany. There, we also attended school. At first, we had temporary accommodation, and then our own flats. The Poles were driven out of their homes, and we moved in. Or they made the flats smaller. We thought we had finally arrived and could stay.

No one thought that we would have to keep moving. We had never eaten so many eggs for Easter. We came to Germany with nothing at all. We got so much food; ten eggs at once on the rations card. That was the rations supply. So much white flour. At first, we received emergency housing. And we set up a large shop window with products. We received so much to eat. But we were afraid. I didn't go with the others when they went to the Hitler Youth. I saw them marching and dressed up at school. And then my mother made friends with the locals. We had so much butter on the food card that we couldn't eat it all. It was given on a sliding scale on the rations card. Up to 12 years old, so much, up to 14 years old, so much, after 14 years, they got so much. They had to grow. That was the German Reich. [laughs] The German Reich had to grow. They brought us clothing that belonged to their sons who had served and fallen. They brought us the clothes, and we gave them butter in return.

How were you treated by the locals? Did you feel completely accepted?

Not at first. Not even at school. They rejected us a bit. But then slowly, we were accepted, and everything was fine. In general, they were very good to us. They felt sorry that we had to go through so much. Many of them felt sorry for us. They brought us things when we needed clothing. They shared with us. They were very kind to us.

Did you notice that the war was going downhill for the Germans?

Yes, that was quite clear. At the beginning of 1944, it might not have been so clear, but afterwards, it was evident. We never thought that after we had been in Germany, we would have to go back. And no one wanted to go back. There came a day in Silesia, on 11 or 12 January, when they drafted my father into the Wehrmacht. But he hardly served at all. That was in January 1945. And they drafted my brother on 26 January. He was 16 years old. They calculated that he was 17 because his birthday was in December of that same year. They sent him to military training for two months to become a soldier. When he returned after two months, my father had already left for the military. My brother had to report to the Wehrmacht within a week, but had one week on leave. And then he had to serve, too. And he went straight to the Front. Our father was lucky while he was in training because the Russians arrived. Then they had to decide where the two of them had to go. Our father went to Berlin and ended up as a prisoner of war with the British, while our family ended up with the Americans.

The Americans captured Leipzig. We went to Rackwitz near Leipzig; 12 kilometres from Leipzig. From there, we fled to the district of Delitzsch. And that's where the Americans took the area under their control.[2] The war was over. The Americans came to us, but the negotiations had already taken place. Berlin was to be divided into four parts and handed over to the Americans, British, French, and Russians according to square metre. But no one was thinking about it. Many of our people left and didn't want to fall to the Russians. They were afraid of the Russians. There were no men left at our home, and our mother didn't dare stay there. We thought that our father and brother would be sent to Russia. And if we were all sent to Russia, maybe we would meet there again. But in Leipzig, there was a lot of short-term work; all the workers were young people. And they didn't want to go back to Russia either.

There was a five-story building in a neighbourhood where only Ukrainians lived. I went there, too. There were two young guys who got to know my sister and had food ration cards. They came with a wagon when the war was almost over. The Americans destroyed everything, and nothing worked anymore. No trains. Nothing. These guys were wandering around and were educated guys. They came to Germany with the German generals in cars. They got wagons and traded. After the war, you had to get a stamp from the town hall. They did all this with the food ration cards. All the guys and girls had to be somehow fed. They asked me to help and wanted to give me something for it. They had an interpreter who rode down on his bike and then shattered his knee. These guys approached the girls, telling them about their business. They then took me with them as an interpreter. Everyone was bartering. I spent the night there. They cooked borscht and Ukrainian food, and sang, and they were all afraid of being sent to Russia. These guys told us they had connections with the Americans. They told us that if the Americans left, they would be informed and taken along. But nobody informed them or us.

One day, someone came riding towards us on a bicycle. Our mother opened the window. The person was riding the bike unevenly. "That must be a Russian. Germans ride straight", our mother said. [laughs] She was absolutely right. It was a Russian. And he came inside. There were many people in this area from the Volga region. They lived very prosperously. They had vineyards and everything. The Russian came in and didn't even realize that they were also Russians. Of course, this happens when you behave properly. "We are at home here", they said. "We have pigs here and grapevines. We want to keep them." The Russian then asked, "Where are you from?" "From such and such a place", was the answer. "Okay, your papers. There are too many of you here."

Then they ordered the men to the detention camp, and none of them wanted to go back to Russia. None of them wanted to go back. There was an old woman who blabbered everything about who was Russian. There are black sheep everywhere. The men were supposed to show up at the camp the next day with their papers and families. The mayor was to provide them with carriages so they could go there. If not, they would be locked up. They were then forced to leave. What could they do? If we had been as wise back then as we are today, we wouldn't have gone. But we were all young boys and didn't have any men at home. The girls who were 19 or 20 years old were the women. My brother was 16, and I was 14. We followed the rules, or else they would have locked us up. That's how it was back then. One by one, they went to the camp.

We arrived in the Ural region after having travelled on a freight train for one or two months. They lied to us, saying that we were going home. Everyone agreed with their signatures to go home. And then they sent us in a freight train with 43 men. We travelled for almost two months without washing and without proper cooking. Sometimes we had to wait at a train station with five trains ahead of us. We couldn't get through. The Wehrmacht was on its way back and had the right of way. We had no opportunity to wash. We had dried potatoes, bread, and dry food. They loaded dry rations into a train car and distributed them to us. They first took us to Brest and unloaded all of us onto a field because the tracks were wider. There were holes everywhere from the bombs. It was a large field. We assembled our suitcases at night so that the Russian soldiers couldn't steal anything. Then they finally put us on another train so that we could continue.

Were you treated like Russians who were on their way home?

No. They saw us as traitors. Like captured traitors. They told us that we had betrayed our homeland. They attached the cars, and we arrived in the Ural on 1 November 1945. We left at the end of September I believe. So, it took about two months. There was immediate frost when we arrived. We didn't have warm clothes from Germany. We nearly froze to death and had to work outside immediately. They didn't let us into the factories. We had so many seriously ill people who died. We weren't allowed to leave the city, or else we would have ended up in prison. We had to sign every month to confirm that we were still there. We had to stay until 1956 when Adenauer arranged for us to go back to Germany. We got an identification card, and then we were able go wherever we wanted.

Denazification by the Church

Wilhelm Blatzheim was a naval radio operator from 1943 to 1945 on board the *Wilhelm Gustloff* and several submarines before receiving orders to dock in Bergen, Norway, where the German Navy surrendered. He returned to his family in 1945 after being held in a British prisoner-of-war camp. He describes his post-war life in Germany.

You needed a work pass after the war in order to get food. And it was difficult to find work because there weren't any jobs. I applied at the regional court, the local court, the district attorney's office – and they wrote back that there wasn't any money or any jobs, but if they had something they would write to me. And one day, I read an article that the director of the municipal waterworks – he lived in Stirzenhof Street – was looking for someone for his office. I applied. They asked me to come to Friesdorfer Street for half a day, with six others who were applying, in order to take a test – maths, writing, and everything that was necessary for it. After the test was over, Director Reich from the waterworks – his son is still a lawyer there today – said: "Mr Blatzheim, I know your father from sport in Bad Godesberg. It looks good for you. I think you'll get the position, but don't say anything to anyone."

I went to my father – to my parents – and they asked: "How was it?" I said: "It looks good. Maybe I'll get the job. That's what they told me, but let's wait and see." Fourteen days later I received a postcard which said: "Dear Mr Blatzheim, we are sorry, but the position has been filled." I told this to my father. And my father said: "I can't understand it. I don't understand it. I'm going to Director Reich. He knows me from the time I was a football player." My father was a well-known football player. And Director Reich didn't want to tell him the reason. My father said: "I have to know what's going on. There must be a reason. You have to give me a reason." Finally, my father was able to convince him and he said: "I can tell you – your son was a member of the NSDAP

[National Socialist German Workers Party] and that your son left the Catholic Church." And my father told me this. I said: "I never was a party member. I also never left the Church." No matter where I applied, I didn't get the job. And afterwards I discovered that my uncle, who was the local Nazi Party group leader, made sure that my name was crossed off the list of Church members. And he signed me up as a member of the NSDAP without my knowledge – without even telling me. The NSDAP no longer existed and there wasn't a signature to go along with it.

But I had to make a formal request to be accepted back into the Church. I was asked to come to Heimbach – to the city of Heimbach – the priest knew me earlier from lessons in school. "Willi, I'm sad that you left the Church", he said. He was a tough guy. In any case, I explained to him what the reason was for this. He said: "Okay, fifty Reichsmarks and the matter will be taken care of. I'll make sure that you're accepted back into the Church, and then you can look for a job in peace." I wanted to thank him and leave, but he said: "Wait! But you still have to say three Our Fathers and three Hail Marys as penance." He stood in front of me and I wanted to begin. "Wait!" he said. "Get down on your knees." I had to follow him on my knees around the long table that seated twelve people while saying the Our Fathers. It was like in a movie. And then he said: "Okay, you've done your penance. Now you decide whether you want to come four times to the High Mass at 10:00 am – you come by the sacristy afterwards and tell me that you were there – or you can go to the early mass four times." Because I liked to sleep late, I thought to myself: "Take the High Mass and then you can sleep longer." I wanted to go to him in the sacristy and tell him that I was at the mass, but he was always busy with local politicians. He was always involved in things. Back then the Church had a great influence on Mayor Hoffmann. I went to church once and then never again. If I felt like it, then I went there. And then one day he actually ran into me in Burg Street where he had his flat and said: "Willi, come here. You didn't report to me." I said: "I was there. Every time that I wanted to talk to you, the sexton threw me out and said that you didn't have any time." He said: "Well, I don't know whether I really believe that." [laughs]

But then my father got me a job at Endemann Real Estate. They were looking for a secretary. They took care of the Association of Property Owners, property management, and real estate. I got eighty Reichsmarks for a fifty-hour week. And I had a work pass and a food ration card that needed to be stamped every month. And one day I was going down Koblenz Street with two good acquaintances, when two men spoke to us in leather coats and hats like they were from the Gestapo. "Excuse us. We have a quick question. Do you have work passes?" they asked. "Yes." "Can we see them?" You always had to have them along. "Yes." We gave them our work passes. And they said: "Okay. We're confiscating them." And shortly afterwards we had to go to the coal mines for three months because they needed a lot of minors. The Russian prisoners of war had been sent home or had died in the meantime. In any case, they needed miners. We were sent to various coal mines near Duisburg for three months with hardly anything to eat and no pay. And my father arranged for me to get there. And from that point on everything was uphill.

Endnotes

Chapter I: National Socialism

1. The Sturmabteilung (Assault Division), commanded by Ernst Röhm, helped to bring Hitler to the power of the chancellery in 1933 through intimidation and murder. Röhm wanted the SA to replace the regular army and operate on an equal footing with the Nazi Party. On 30 June 1934 (also known as the Night of the Long Knives), Hitler used the SS to purge the ranks of the SA and to murder Röhm. After this purge, the SA was considerably reduced in size and ceased to play a major role in Nazi political politics. Starting in 1939, the SA was responsible for training able-bodied men for Home Guard units.
2. The Deutsche Christen (DC) were a group within the Protestant church that actively supported the Nazi Party. In 1933, they played a key role in merging twenty-nine regional churches into the Protestant Reich Church and influenced the election of Ludwig Müller, one of Hitler's confidants, as Reich Bishop. They called for abolishing the Old Testament and removing Jewish influence from the Church. Their emblem featured a swastika in the centre of a traditional Christian cross.
3. After the establishment of the Reich Church in 1933, Pastor Martin Niemöller asserted that the Bekennende Kirche (Confessing Church) he led was the legitimate Protestant church of Germany. In response, Hitler ordered the arrest of Confessing Church members and the confiscation of their funds. In 1937, Pastor Niemöller was arrested by the Gestapo and imprisoned in the camps at Sachsenhausen and Dachau. Later, he was transferred to Tyrol, where Allied forces freed him the end of the war.

4. The Deutsches Jungvolk (German Young Folk) was a youth organization in Nazi Germany for boys aged 10 to 14. It was succeeded by the Hitlerjugend (Hitler Youth) for boys aged 15 to 18 as pre-military training. The Jungmädel (Young Girls) and Bund Deutscher Mädel (League of German Girls) were the respective youth organizations for girls in Nazi Germany.
5. The Goldenes Parteiabzeichen (Golden Party Badge) was established by a decree from Hitler in 1933 for party members who had been actively registered since 1925 and whose membership number was below 100,000.
6. When Hitler was imprisoned after the Munich Beer Hall Putsch, Alfred Rosenberg temporarily assumed leadership of the Nazi Party. Rosenberg advocated the conquest of Poland and Russia and argued in favour of the purity of the German race. At the Nuremberg Trials, he was convicted as a war criminal and executed by hanging.
7. Martin Bormann served as the head of the Nazi press in Thuringia (Saxony) from 1926 to 1928. In 1933, he became chief of staff to Rudolf Hess, the deputy Führer. After Hess's infamous flight to Scotland in 1941, Bormann assumed the role of the head of administration in the Nazi Party, gaining control of legislation, party promotions, and appointments. At the Nuremberg Trials, he was sentenced to death in absentia.
8. Albert Speer was the Third Reich's chief architect and designed numerous parade grounds used for Nazi Party rallies. In 1942, he became Minister of Armaments and Munitions and his authority extended to raw materials and industrial production which involved the use of slave labour in concentration camps. At the Nuremberg Trials, he confessed his guilt and served a twenty-year sentence in Spandau Prison in West Berlin. Afterwards, he wrote several books about his participation in the Nazi Party.
9. The Ahnenpass (family ancestry book) was required of all German citizens in the Third Reich to prove their pure Aryan family lineage.
10. Abd al-Aziz ibn Saud was the king of Saudi Arabia from 1932 to 1953.
11. On the Reichskristallnacht (9 and 10 November 1938), named for the broken glass left in the aftermath, Jewish businesses and

synagogues were vandalized throughout Germany. The Gestapo arrested 30,000 wealthy Jews, who were released on the condition that they surrender their wealth to the Nazis and emigrate from the country.

12. The Gestapo headquarters was named after the jeweller Leopold Dahmen (hence the German pronunciation of the initials LD) from whom the Nazis originally rented the building. It survived Allied bombings during the war and today houses the National Socialism Documentation Centre.
13. The prestigious Blood Order was awarded to original party members who participated in the Munich Beer Hall Putsch on 9 November 1923, when 2,000 followers of Adolf Hitler attempted to seize control of the Bavarian state through clashes with the police. Hermann Göring was seriously injured, and Adolf Hitler was sentenced to prison in Landsberg Fortress, where he wrote *Mein Kampf* and served only nine months.
14. The Stuka (Sturzkampfflugzeug) was a single-engine dive-bomber that could reach a maximum speed of 340 kilometres per hour and had the ability to break while diving, giving the pilot more time to aim at the target. It terrified people on the ground with its screeching noise during dives.
15. Originally, the runic alphabet was used by Germanic peoples in northern Europe from the third to the seventeenth century AD. The Nazis adopted the lightning-like runic SS characters as an abbreviation for the Schutzstaffel (the Nazi's black-uniformed elite corps).
16. The "Horst Wessel Song" was the anthem of Nazi Germany. It was named after the SA member, Horst Wessel, who was killed by political enemies and subsequently elevated to martyrdom by the propagandist Josef Goebbels.
17. Baron Otmar von Verschuer was the editor of the journal *Erbarzt* (*The Genetic Doctor*) beginning in 1934 and director of the Kaiser Wilhelm Institute of Anthropology in the 1940s. Although he was never formally charged with war crimes, he served as the doctoral supervisor of Josef Mengele at the University of Frankfurt. Mengele allegedly continued many of Verschuer's genetic experiments with twins in Auschwitz and Birkenau.

Chapter II: Allied Bombings

1. The Siegfried Line was Germany's western defence line in WWII, extending nearly 630 kilometres parallel to the Rhine with 18,000 bunkers, tunnels, and tank traps.
2. German Federal Minister of Economics from 1977 to 1982 and again from 1982 to 1984.

Chapter III: Retreat from the East

1. The *Wilhelm Gustloff* was struck by three torpedoes from the Soviet submarine S-13 while crossing the Baltic Sea on the night of 30 January1945. The ship sank along with 9,400 passengers.

Chapter IV: The Russian Invasion

1. The Armed SS (Waffen-SS), a multinational military force under the control of the SS, served as the protective arm of the Schutzstaffel and fought alongside the regular German Army throughout World War II.
2. Panjewagons were long, lightweight, horse-drawn carts used by the German military in the East. The carts derived their name from the Polish word for "lord" or "master" and entered German vocabulary during World War I on the Eastern Front.

Chapter VI: Aftermath of the War

1. According to accounts from ethnic German survivors, Maltheuern was established as a Czech concentration camp towards the end of the war. This camp, consisting of hutted structures and surrounded by barbed wire, housed a fluctuating population estimated at 500 to 1,300 individuals, primarily men. Within its confines, German

prisoners endured systematic humiliation, torture, and acts of violence, often resulting in fatalities.

2. The military operations in Delitzsch concluded on 18 April 1945, predating the formal surrender of the Third Reich in May 1945 to the Allied forces. On 20 April 1945, American troops peacefully occupied the city from the southwest without encountering resistance or suffering any casualties on either side. The Red Army subsequently replaced the US Army in early July 1945 and maintained a presence in the area until the mid-1950s. Many factories were dismantled and transported to the Soviet Union as reparations.

Index